the latest

SERIES

SOUTHWARK
remembered

'10

10

004

One wall of Marshalsea Prison can still be seen outside Southwark Local Studies Library, built on the site of the prison well-known to Charles Dickens. The prison closed in 1842 but much of the first part of *Little Dorrit* revolves around it. In 1856 Dickens wrote: 'Thirty years ago there stood, a few doors on the left-hand side of the way going southward, the Marshalsea Prison. It had stood there many years before and remained there some years afterwards, but it is gone now and the world is none the worse without it… Itself a close and confined prison for debtors, it contained within it a much closer and more confined gaol for smugglers.' The photograph shows the wall of Marshalsea Prison in 1887. The Marshalsea Prison pump can be seen in the Cuming Museum in Walworth Road.

Changing Times
SERIES

SOUTHWARK

remembered

Compiled by
John D. Beasley

TEMPUS

First published 2001
Copyright © John D. Beasley, 2001

Tempus Publishing Limited
The Mill, Brimscombe Port,
Stroud, Gloucestershire, GL5 2QG

ISBN 0 7524 2241 3

Typesetting and origination by
Tempus Publishing Limited
Printed in Great Britain by
Midway Colour Print, Wiltshire

Cover picture: The Elephant and Castle junction in 1889 showing the Elephant and Castle public house to the left and Newington Butts receding to the right.

Acknowledgements

If countless people, known and unknown, had not recorded information and taken photographs this book could not have been produced. Apart from expressing appreciation for those people, I must thank Len Reilly, Librarian at Southwark Local Studies Library, for his assistance and co-operation; Stephen Humphrey, archivist, who checked all the articles before they were sent to the *South London Press*; Steve Potter and Lynne Kendall for additional assistance in the library which I enjoy visiting every week.

Stephen Humphrey is an expert on Southwark and churches in England. His books include *Southwark, Bermondsey and Rotherhithe in Old Photographs*; *Camberwell, Dulwich and Peckham in Old Photographs*; *Southwark: The Twentieth Century* and *Churches and Cathedrals of London*.

As usual, I appreciate Gill Frost (treasurer of The Peckham Society) making many helpful comments on the typescript and reading the proofs. In addition, I am grateful to Derek Austin, Rob Bowden (former editor of the *South London Press* who commissioned me to write the Memory Lane articles), Ernest Coup (William Booth College), Pam Elven, Harold and Sheila Franklin, Gill Griffiths (William Booth College), Martin Harrison-Putnam, assistant curator of London's Transport Museum (for the picture of the steam bus garage), Trudi Hayes, assistant curator of the London Fire Brigade Museum (for the picture of Winchester House), Lucy McQuillin (Peabody Trust), Dr Mary Mills (editor, *London's Industrial Archaeology*), Peter Morris (who enjoys the Memory Lane articles in the *South London Press* and encouraged me to find a publisher so they could reach a wider audience), Dennis G. Plowright, Bob Smyth (for the picture of Watkins' Bible factory), The Camberwell Society, *The Times* (for the picture of Geraldine Mary Harmsworth Park), Tibet Foundation, Dave Twydell of Yore Publications (for the picture used on the cover of *Nunhead Football Club 1888-1949*), Christine Wagg (Peabody Trust), Hannah Walker (editor, *South London Press*, who readily agreed to the articles being reproduced in a book), Robert Whitten and Ron Woollacott (chairman, Friends of Nunhead Cemetery).

4

Contents

Bermondsey Workhouse in Tanner Street was decorated in 1911 for the coronation of George V. Children from that workhouse were sent to a children's home and school in Shirley near Croydon. The story of that establishment is told in *Shirley Oaks Children's Home* by Jad Adams and Gerry Coll.

Other local history books by John D. Beasley:

Building Together: The Story of Peckham Methodist Church
Peckham Methodist Church, Wood's Road, London SE15 2PX
Who Was Who in Peckham
Chener Books Ltd, 14 Lordship Lane, London SE22 8HN
The Bitter Cry Heard and Heeded:
The Story of the South London Mission of the Methodist Church 1889-1989
South London Mission, Central Hall, Bermondsey Street, London SE1 3UJ
Peckham and Nunhead Churches
South Riding Press, 6 Everthorpe Road, London SE15 4DA
Peckham Rye Park Centenary
South Riding Press
Transport in Peckham and Nunhead
South Riding Press
East Dulwich: An Illustrated Alphabetical Guide
South Riding Press
The Story of Peckham and Nunhead
Southwark Local Studies Library, 211 Borough High Street, London SE1 1JA
The Images of England Series: Peckham and Nunhead
Tempus Publishing, Brimscombe Port, Stroud, GL5 2QG
Changing Times Series: Peckham and Nunhead Remembered
Tempus Publishing
Changing Times Series: East Dulwich Remembered
Tempus Publishing

Introduction

A painting hangs in the Museum of London called *London from Southwark*; it was painted by an unknown artist around 1630 and can be seen on the cover of *The Story of Bankside*. In the picture the old St Paul's Cathedral dominates the landscape with the old London Bridge to the east. On the south side of the Thames can be seen The Swan Theatre, The Hope Theatre, The Rose Theatre, Globe Theatre, Winchester House, Church of St Saviour (which became Southwark Cathedral), Nonsuch House, Gateway with traitors' heads and Church of St Olave. All these buildings stood in what today is the London Borough of Southwark, formed in 1965 when the Metropolitan Boroughs of Bermondsey, Camberwell and Southwark were amalgamated. These three boroughs were amalgamations of the ancient civil parishes of Christ Church, Blackfriars Road; Saint Saviour; Saint Thomas; Saint Olave; Saint George the Martyr; Saint Mary, Newington; Saint John, Horselydown; Saint Mary Magdalen, Bermondsey; Saint Mary, Rotherhithe, and Saint Giles, Camberwell. Until the London County Council was formed in 1889, all these parishes were in the County of Surrey.

The London Borough of Southwark is described by the London Tourist Board as London's most historic borough, and people have been living there since before the Romans invaded Britain. Materials found suggest that an Iron Age settlement was present in Southwark possibly making Southwark the South Bank's oldest residential area of London. The borough is seething with fascinating history which is why the *South London Press* includes pictorial articles on Southwark in its Friday edition. This book has been produced by using articles which have been published in that newspaper since 1997.

John D. Beasley
June 2001

Southwark Local Studies Library

The author is grateful to Southwark Local Studies Library which has an excellent collection of books, documents, cuttings and photographs covering the whole of the London Borough of Southwark. The library, close to the historic St George the Martyr Church and Borough Underground Station, is at No. 211 Borough High Street, SE1 1JA (020 7403 3507). Among the many publications for sale are these published by the library:

Illustrated pocket histories of the communities within the London Borough of Southwark:

The Story of Bankside by Geoff Marshall and Leonard Reilly £4
The Story of Bermondsey by Mary Boast £1.95
The Story of The Borough by Mary Boast £1.95
The Story of Camberwell by Mary Boast £3.50
The Story of Dulwich by Mary Boast £2
The Story of Peckham and Nunhead by John D. Beasley £3.50
The Story of Rotherhithe by Stephen Humphrey £3.50
The Story of Walworth by Mary Boast £3

Southwark: an illustrated history by Leonard Reilly. Lavishly illustrated with over 100 views, many in colour. £6.95
Below Southwark by Carrie Cowan. Shows the story of Southwark as revealed by excavations over the last thirty years. £4.95
Southwark in Archives by Stephen Humphrey. A well-illustrated introduction to the archives held at Southwark Local Studies Library. £4.95
Southwark Park by Pat Kingwell et al. An illustrated book on one of London's earliest municipal parks. £1.95
The Southwark Trail Three historical walks around Bankside, Borough High Street and Bermondsey. £1.95
Charles Dickens and Southwark by Graham Prettejohns et al. £2.50

In Southwark Local Studies Library the *South London Press* can be seen on microfilm from its first issue in 1865.

Evacuees returned to the Oliver Goldsmith School dispersal point in Peckham Road in June 1945 after the end of the Second World War. Thus came to an end years away from home for many mothers and children who reacted in different ways to the experience.

One person has written: 'We all thought there was going to be a full-scale war, panic stations. We all got ready to go away. When they announced it - they were evacuating us to Rye - I was on Denmark Hill station and all of us were crying our eyes out. We'd all had to pack our bags for twelve o'clock. We were waiting to get on a train and before we got on we heard the siren go. They thought they were going to come over right away and start bombing, so they bundled us all in the train and we didn't have time to say goodbye or anything. We were all pushed into the train and off we went. We didn't know where we were going. All the signs were all wiped out. You didn't know where you were. You couldn't say anything because if you opened your mouth you didn't know who was listening.'

Local government affairs for the parish of St Giles in Camberwell were run by the Vestry in the nineteenth century. The first Vestry Hall was built in 1827 on the opposite corner of Havil Street from the present Southwark Town Hall. A much larger Vestry Hall was erected in 1872/73. When Camberwell became a Metropolitan Borough in 1900, this became the Town Hall. The Vestry Hall was rebuilt in 1934 but the Council of the London Borough of Southwark meet in the Council Chamber of the former Vestry Hall.

A horse parade is seen outside the baths and wash-houses in Manor Place, Walworth, in 1912. Local authorities possessed many horses in the nineteenth and early twentieth centuries, and parades were held annually.

One

Commerce

The Docks

Greenland Dock is seen here with ships surrounded by barges, a characteristic practice of the Port of London which came about because of the long-standing influence of lightermen. When the enclosed wet docks were formed at the end of the eighteenth century, pressure from the lightermen led to the insertion of the 'free-water clause' into the Acts of Parliament for building the docks. This enabled lighters (or barges) to enter the docks without charge. Many ships in the Port of London therefore unloaded their cargo into barges, for removal to warehouses upstream, rather than onto the quays of the docks themselves. Unlike some of the other Surrey Commercial Docks, Greenland Dock still exists and is used by the Surrey Docks Watersports Centre.

Greenland Dock, c. 1925.

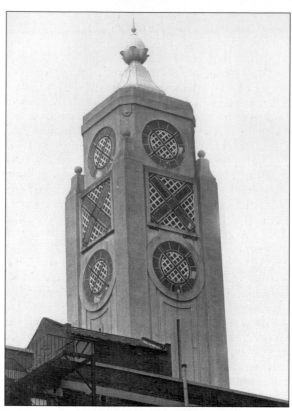

The Oxo Tower, 1979. The letters in the sign are over 10ft wide and the tower is 202 ft tall.

The Oxo Tower

The history of Oxo Tower Wharf, which stands on the south bank of the Thames close to Blackfriars Bridge, goes back to 1927. In that year the Liebig Extract of Meat Company, which produced Oxo, formed a subsidiary company, Thames Side Properties Ltd, to deal with the purchase and use of a site for a new wharf. The company was looking for a new site as the lease on their existing River Plate Wharf at Limehouse was due to expire in 1930. A new wharf was therefore built on the site of the GPO power station; it had 9 floors and a floor space of 250,000 square feet. The building was made from reinforced concrete which had to be capable of holding 4 cwts to a square foot.

The first mention of a tower was made in 1929, and when it was built it was the second tallest building in London. Once it was decided to add a tower, there were planning regulations to overcome so that the Oxo sign was not classified as an advertisement as it was not allowed at that height. It was therefore decided to illuminate the windows shaped in the form of the letters OXO, so that the light shone through the windows to form Oxo shapes. Apparently, the company did receive instructions to pull down the tower, but these could not be enforced. In 1931 the company chairman said: 'The Oxo Tower attracts universal attention and admiration, particularly when illuminated at night time, and is considered to be of great value as an advertising feature.'

In 1983 there was a campaign to save the tower as it was threatened with demolition as part of a new building development scheme.

Lime Kiln

All that remains of Burtt's Limeworks which opened in 1816, soon after the Grand Surrey Canal was built, is an old lime kiln, preserved in Burgess Park. In those days bulk raw materials were delivered to the kiln by barge. The kiln was used to heat limestone and convert it into quicklime needed for the cement that was in great demand as the area became increasingly built up with houses and other buildings. The kiln is one of few reminders of how this part of north Camberwell looked before Burgess Park was created.

While all other major parks in London were made by defending the land against the encroachment of building development, roads and railways, at Burgess Park the process was reversed. Where once there were factories, churches, streets and around 2,000 houses, there are now 130 acres of open space. In 1943 planners saw the opportunity to create out of an expanse of bombed and demolition sites a large park. North Camberwell Open Space, as it was originally called, was started in 1950. The park grew as more houses were demolished and the canal was filled in.

The environmental charity Groundwork Southwark is working energetically to improve Burgess Park which was named after Cllr Jessie Burgess, Camberwell's first woman mayor (1945-1947). For forty-four years she served on Camberwell Council and Southwark Council.

Apart from the lime kiln, other reminders of the nineteenth century in the park are a footbridge which crossed the canal, St George's church (opened in 1824) and Chumleigh Gardens (almshouses erected in 1821 by the Friendly Female Society). E.R. Burtt & Sons and the lime kiln are featured in *The Story of Burgess Park* by Tim Charlesworth.

Old lime kiln, 1930.

Samuel Jones' gummed paper factory, Peckham Grove, *c.* 1960.

Gummed Paper

A Camberwell Beauty butterfly made from coloured tiles can be seen on the side of the former wash-house in Wells Way. It was removed from the top of the Samuel Jones factory in Peckham Grove before it was demolished in 1982. The gummed paper firm adopted the Camberwell Beauty as its trademark in 1912 because Edward Jones, a grandson of the founder, was interested in entomology. The butterfly was first recorded in England in 1748 when two specimens were captured in what is now Coldharbour Lane when Camberwell was a Surrey village.

Samuel Jones was born in 1818 and entered his father's stationery firm when he was thirteen. He succeeded to the business in 1845. In 1865 Samuel purchased Nos 67-69 Peckham Grove and three years later erected a small factory at the bottom of his garden at No. 67. These houses became part of the site for the factory which was completed in 1920.

In 1874 Samuel Jones retired and his son James took the firm over but continued to trade under the name of his father. Six years later the first hand gumming of paper in the sheet was commenced. In 1886 gumming of paper in reel form was started. In 1924 the firm was awarded the contract for gumming British postage stamps so new premises were opened at Watford to do this work.

Samuel was a religious man who wrote *The Pliable of the Nineteenth Century brought to the Bar of Eternal Truth.* An autograph copy is preserved in Southwark Local Studies Library.

Jam

Hartley's jam factory has been converted into flats and offices but the building is still a reminder of an important aspect of Bermondsey's history. Mr W.P. Hartley achieved a great reputation as a manufacturer of preserves at Aintree, Liverpool. His new factory at Green Walk, Bermondsey was opened on Tuesday 25 June 1901 by Mr H.C. Cust MP in the presence of the mayor of Bermondsey. A report of the opening ceremony was published in the *South London Press* four days later. Mr Hartley said that electricity would be used for both power and light; at that time gas was the main fuel for lighting people's homes.

The factory was established with a view to extending the firm's trade in marmalade and jam, and covered 2 acres at a cost of £100,000. The factory contained over 1,500,000 cubic feet. In view of possible fires, the largest building allowed by the London County Council was 250,000 cubic feet. To meet the council's requirements, strong walls and fireproof doors were installed to divide the huge building into seven or eight departments. Facilities were provided for loading and unloading between fifteen and twenty vans at a time, all on Mr Hartley's land without encroaching on the public street. The jams and marmalades were produced from fresh fruit and filled in highly glazed stoneware jars which were stacked in the huge warehouses until sold.

Mr Hartley looked after the welfare of his workforce and ran a profit-sharing scheme.

Delivery drivers outside Hartley's jam factory, *c.* 1921.

The former Hop and Malt Exchange, 1931.

The Hop Exchange

For much of the twentieth century, hop picking in Kent was a common way for hundreds of families from Southwark and Bermondsey to spend the summer months. The former Hop and Malt Exchange, originally opened in 1867, still stands in Southwark Street. It was designed by R.H. Moore and had a glass roof so that the quality of the hops could be examined in good natural light. In the front, Portland stone pedestals formed the base of cast-iron ornamental columns; these extended the whole length of the building. Around the Exchange were four storeys of offices and showrooms. The three upper floors were approached from ornamental cast-iron galleries running all the way around.

By erecting the Exchange, hop growers, merchants, dealers and buyers had the advantages of a complete and well-attended market, close to the termini of all the railways which passed through the hop growing districts of Kent, Surrey and Sussex. In the immediate vicinity there were numerous hop merchants' warehouses including Calvert's Buildings across the road.

Unfortunately extensive damage to the Exchange was caused by a fire in 1920. Two upper floors had to be removed and the building was converted into offices called Central Buildings. In recent years its name has reverted to the Hop Exchange and it has undergone a creditable restoration. The great hall inside – the exchange floor – is Southwark's least known important Victorian interior.

Friern Manor Farm

Friern Road and surrounding Victorian streets in East Dulwich were built on farmland. Friern Farm was a farm in the Middle Ages run for Halliwell Priory at Shoreditch. An article on the farm as it was nearly 150 years ago was published in *The Illustrated London News* on 11 June 1853 and began: 'The supply of milk to the London market is so important a branch of commerce, that an account of one of the largest dairy farms in the Metropolis may be read with interest.'

The farm had no fewer than 186 cows which were kept in sheds, lit by gas. One held 50 cows. Fourteen people were employed to do the milking and the average time spent milking each cow was seven minutes. The cows seemed to regard their milk with 'a strange kind of maternal pride' for none of them liked to be milked into a pail containing milk from any other cow. Each cow was humoured by having a pail to herself. If this regulation was ignored by the milker the cow was likely to kick over the pail which contained the milk of another cow. The milking took place twice a day starting at 1.30 a.m. and 10.30 a.m. The milk reached London at 5 a.m. and 1 p.m. respectively.

The pleasant meadows of Friern Manor Estate were put up for auction in 1864, the farm materials were sold in 1873 and by two years later roads had been laid across most of the ancient fields.

Drawing of the cow shed at Friern Manor Dairy Farm, 1853.

The old headquarters of Thomas Tilling's omnibus firm in Peckham High Street, 1953.

Thomas Tilling's Omnibuses

Winchester House, which stood at the corner of Peckham High Street and the east side of Sumner Road, was still in existence in 1953. It had been the headquarters of Thomas Tilling's omnibus firm. Before that it was a grammar school where the founder's son, Richard S. Tilling, was educated. During a lesson Richard scratched his initials R.S.T. on a window pane with a glass-cutter; Thomas Tilling later worked in this old schoolroom, which was known as 'the parlour'. This room became the heart of the business; all the important decisions were made there.

When the cellars of this old building were altered in 1915 an underground passage was discovered which had long connected Winchester House with the property across the road, Basing Manor House (demolished in 1883). Winchester House had a front garden which was destroyed when the road was widened.

Thomas Tilling started his four-horse omnibus service from Rye Lane to Oxford Circus in 1851, the year of the Great Exhibition at Hyde Park. His was the fastest on the route. He was the first proprietor to refuse to pick up passengers from various places and take them to the omnibus starting point, nor would he wait until the omnibus was full before it set off.

Murals on the former North Peckham Civic Centre, in the Old Kent Road, and the Nunhead Green Community Centre include a Tilling omnibus. At London's Transport Museum in Covent Garden one of *The Times* omnibuses used by Thomas Tilling is preserved. Thomas was buried in Nunhead Cemetery where his grave can still be seen.

Printing and Binding

Burgess Park was created on land where houses, factories and other buildings were erected in the nineteenth century. In Cowan Street, close to Chumleigh Gardens, Watkins' Book Binding Factory stood between terraced houses. The firm bound Bibles for the British and Foreign Bible Society and was one of the last businesses in the area to use a horse and cart. The general foreman, Jess Byfield, still rode a bicycle to work when he was eighty; after arriving, he changed into a silk jacket. The factory was bombed during the Second World War but was rebuilt. The firm then closed down in 1977.

Watkins, Watkins & Co Ltd, as the firm was officially known, did binding and not printing. The first printer of an English Bible in England was James Nicholson of Southwark. During the sixteenth century he printed an edition of the Coverdale Bible. The wording on the imprint stated: 'Imprynted in Southwarke, in saint Thomas hospitale, by James Nycolson 1537'. Southwark therefore gained unique distinction in both Church and typographic history.

In 1546 the use of Coverdale's New Testament was forbidden by royal decree. Under Edward VI this policy was reversed by the Protestant movement and the English versions were again reprinted. The year 1537 was marked by the issue from Nicholson's printing office of several other works. Chief among these was a Coverdale translation of Martin Luther's Bible and various volumes on religious themes. Two undated books are believed to have been produced by him in that year. These various items, added to two editions of the Coverdale Bible, represent an output which can be regarded as formidable.

Watkins' Book Binding factory in 1976.

B. Young's factory seen from the air.

Gelatin

Gelatin was made in Bermondsey by B. Young & Co. Ltd who occupied a site at No. 123 Grange Road. The firm was formed as a private company in 1884 and changed its status to a limited company in 1906. Later it acquired the adjacent glue and size works known as Proctor and Bevington.

In 1920 a company known as British Glue & Chemicals Ltd was formed by the amalgamation of seven existing companies engaged in the glue and gelatin trade. This was done to strengthen their position against German and Austrian competition. This company bought B. Young & Co. Ltd in 1926.

B. Young & Co. Ltd traded under its own name and was engaged in the manufacture of gelatin, producing edible, photographic, pharmaceutical and technical grades. The total annual production averaged about 3,500 tons. The bulk of the production was low-grade edible gelatin known as 'Spa' gelatin (shades of the long gone Bermondsey Spa, which gave the name to Spa Road). Around 500 tons per annum of photographic gelatin were made and this was used for coating films, X-ray plates and photographic paper.

The manufacture of gelatin in the 1950s was a labour intensive operation and used mostly manual skills. About 250 people were employed on the site; most of them lived locally.

By around 1960 British Glues and Chemicals Ltd had been taken over by Croda Ltd. When the factory closed in 1981 production was transferred to Widnes. The site was sold in 1982 for a housing development and all traces of B. Young & Co. Ltd have vanished.

Jones and Higgins' Store

Jones and Higgins in Rye Lane was a major store in South London until it closed in 1980. The Aylesham Centre now occupies most of the site though the tower still exists. The tower was built by 1896 but the top part was rebuilt after it was damaged during the Second World War.

The department store was founded by Edwin Jones and George Randell Higgins. They became apprentices to an old-established business for the sum of £12 a year. By 1867 the two young men had saved enough money to open a small draper's shop at No. 1 Coburn Terrace, later known as No. 3 Rye Lane. Their first week's takings were £13 19s 4d. In the early days Mr Jones and Mr Higgins slept under the counters of the shop to save lodging fees.

The firm expanded quite rapidly, and in 1896 it was converted into a limited liability company. By 1923 it was employing 1,000 members of staff. George Randell Higgins' son, and then his grandson, succeeded him in the business which continued in the family until 1954 when it was taken over by Great Universal Stores. After Jones and Higgins' department store closed down on 7 June 1980, it was reopened two days later as The Houndsditch in Peckham. It was then demolished in 1985.

Edwin Jones represented Peckham as a Progressive on the London County Council. He donated a drinking fountain to Peckham Rye Park.

Jones and Higgins' store, c. 1910.

Geo. Carter and Sons.

George Carter and Sons

George Carter & Sons Ltd was a well-known men's clothing shop in the Old Kent Road until it closed in 1978. It was during the year of the Great Exhibition in Hyde Park in 1851 that George Carter founded his business in a four-roomed cottage in Russell Place, Old Kent Road. He made silk hats for the wholesale trade and soon had to move to a larger house at No. 215 Old Kent Road. It was not until he erected a showcase in the front garden that the retail business was started. As the business grew, bigger premises were needed so a shop was built and in 1867 the house and shop were made into one.

With characteristic ingenuity, George Carter devised coins the shape, colour and size of a gold sovereign. On the front, in regal serenity, appeared the bearded face in profile of George Carter. On the obverse was stamped his trade mark. Mr Carter used to throw handfuls of these mock coins from the tops of the two-horse trams and omnibuses to the delight of crowds of small boys who scrambled for them in the road. One of the coins was found among the rubble in the Old Kent Road during the Second World War after a heavy air raid.

Fifty years after George Carter started his business, the firm had over thirty branches, a factory and a warehouse. Although the business started as a hatters, its scope was soon extended to include hosiery, gloves and shirts as well as clothing. In 1904 the son of the founder used to cut his own caps in his spare time. The story of George Carter & Sons is told in *Old Surviving Firms of South London* by Steven Harris.

Austin's

Austin's at Peckham Rye was one of the largest antique and second-hand dealers in Europe. The firm was started by George Austin (1844-1925) who was born in the Oxfordshire village of Blackthorn. He moved to London and by 1876 had opened Oxford Farm Dairy at No. 39 Brayards Road.

When the milk round was finished he used the milk cart for small household removals. Billheads in the 1880s advertised: 'Cows kept for Infants and Invalids – Milking hours 5 till 7 a.m., 1 till 3 p.m.' The same billheads showed an illustration of a horse-drawn furniture van and advertised 'Household Removals – Furniture Warehoused'. In 1905 the Peckham Rye site was acquired.

George Austin served on the Camberwell Vestry from 1894 until the Vestry was superseded by Camberwell Borough Council; he served on that for three years.

George Edward Austin, son of the firm's founder, with his four sons built the business to international recognition in the 1930s. Derek Austin, George's great grandson, joined the firm in 1949 after demobilisation as a pilot in the RAF. A decade later he was joined by his sister Valerie. They ran the famous store until it closed in 1994 as they were unable to find anyone to continue the business.

The list of show business personalities and Royals who were clients reads like *Who's Who*. Among the customers were actors – David Niven, Sean Connery, Maggie Smith, Rex Harrison, Yvonne de Carlo and June Whitfield; writers – Muriel Spark, Elizabeth Jane Howard and Beryl Bainbridge; theatre designer Cecil Beaton and singer Shirley Bassey. Royalty included Princess Margaret and Princess Beatrix who is Queen of the Netherlands.

Austins Court now occupies the site of the firm's premises.

George Austin outside Oxford Farm Dairy, *c.* 1910.

Peek Frean's biscuit factory, c. 1960.

Peek Frean's Biscuits

Peek Frean's biscuit factory in Bermondsey no longer exists but it is remembered by many local people. The first Mr Peek was a partner in the firm of Peek Bros., tea merchants in the City of London. He had two sons, Charles and Edward. To his great disappointment, his sons refused to follow him in his own business. Since they had to do something, he decided to set them up in another business which would be more congenial and which one day they would own.

Down in the West Country lived George Hender Frean, a miller and ships' biscuit maker, who had married one of Peek's nieces. Peek wrote to him asking why he did not come to London. He explained that if he would do so, he would help to finance a biscuit factory for Charles and Edward. Frean should manage it and have a partnership in it. That was how in 1857 the firm of Peek Frean began in Mill Street, Bermondsey. Unfortunately nothing went right. The Peek sons decided that they had no more liking for the biscuit business than for tea. Charles left, went into the provinces and died. Edward forsook trade for the Church.

Despite various difficulties, Peek refused to give in. In 1862 a bronze medal was won at the International Exhibition held in London. This was for a variety of steam-made biscuits but the marked turn of fortune came three years later when the famous Pearl biscuit was produced. This was the pioneer of the modern biscuit – it was mixed and made differently. New varieties of biscuits were produced and a ten-acre site was bought in 1866 in Drummond Road so a new factory could be built.

Two
Education and Libraries

Dulwich Grammar School

The Old Grammar School in Dulwich stands at the corner of Burbage Road and Gallery Road, and was designed by Charles Barry who also designed the Houses of Parliament. It stands as the most important memorial to his twenty-eight years as surveyor and architect to the Dulwich College Estate. The building is elegant but rather plain in the Tudor Gothic style, with gables and a door with Gothic lettering and coat of arms.

The Grammar School was built in 1841 and opened the following year. Sixty boys were admitted and divided into two classes, an upper and a lower school, separated by a wooden partition. The upper school later became Dulwich College. The upper boys paid 4 guineas a year and the lower boys 2d a week. The original twelve poor scholars continued to be instructed as before in the old College.

When the College was reformed in 1857 the twelve poor scholars were incorporated into the lower school. Later the upper school moved into the west wing of the College leaving the Grammar School entirely for the use of the lower school until it became Alleyn's School and moved to its new premises in 1887. The Grammar School building then became the Village Reading Room.

The Old Grammar School in Dulwich. It was designed by Charles Barry in the nineteenth century and is seen here in the early part of the twentieth century.

Dulwich College, 1951.

The College of God's Gift

Dulwich College was founded by actor Edward Alleyn on 21 June 1619 with a licence from King James I; a splendid document with the Great Seal of England is preserved at the College. Alleyn (1566-1626) was a colourful and famous figure. By 1600 he was part owner and manager of the Fortune Theatre, the main rival of the Globe Theatre. In 1605 Alleyn bought the manorial estate of Dulwich for £35,000 from Sir Francis Calton. He later decided to build a college which would help both old people and poor children. It was to be a home for twelve old people, what Alleyn called 'six poor brothers and sisters' and a boys' school for 'twelve poor scholars'. The Old College still stands in the centre of Dulwich at the junction of College Road and Gallery Road and the east wing is still in use as almshouses.

Most children never had a chance to go to school in the seventeenth century so there was a competition to be chosen as a 'poor scholar'. When two boys had been selected they had to draw lots from two pieces of paper. The one who chose the piece with 'God's Gift' written on it had a place at the College. That is why it was called 'The College of God's Gift in Dulwich'.

Dulwich College grew and needed much bigger premises. By selling some land to the railway companies, the College raised enough money to build a new college. The architect of the new College buildings was Charles Barry Jnr. The new College was opened in 1870.

The Datchelor Sisters

Save the Children Fund is based in Mary Datchelor House in Grove Lane, Camberwell. The building used to be Mary Datchelor School. The school opened in 1877 and stood on the site of a medieval manor house which had a history dating back to the time of the Domesday Book in 1086.

During the eighteenth century three sisters – Mary, Beatrix and Sarah Datchelor – left money to the 'poor inhabitants' near their home in Threadneedle Street in the City of London. However by the next century the area was prosperous and no longer needed the bequest. In 1871 the Charity Commissioners allowed the Datchelor Charity to establish a girls' school in Camberwell with £20,000 from the Trust.

The school's first headmistress was Miss Caroline Edith Rigg who served from 1877 to 1917. Her father was Dr James Harrison Rigg who was Principal of Westminster College. The headmistress had to have 'considerable administrative and intellectual abilities, and great tact and patient firmness'.

When the school opened it had 30 pupils aged between eight and sixteen. Four years later there were 324 pupils. One school inspector stated that other schools should follow the example set by Mary Datchelor School as its standards were so high. The pupils worked from 9 a.m. until 3 p.m. and had only 30 minutes for lunch.

By 1881 new classrooms, a hall, library and museum were added to the school. In 1894 the Clothworkers' Company acquired the school. In 1939 the school with its head, Dame Dorothy Brock, was evacuated to Ashford in Kent. The school closed in 1981.

Mary Datchelor School, c. 1905.

William Booth College, c. 1935.

William Booth College

The tower of William Booth College is a landmark which can be seen many miles away from Denmark Hill. The Salvation Army were determined to have a tower that would rise as high as the cross on the top of St Paul's Cathedral. They wanted it to be permanently illuminated and shine over the slums of London. Unfortunately the tower was not finished for the opening of the college on 8 July 1929 in the centennial year of William Booth's birth. HRH Prince George, later the Duke of Kent, performed the opening ceremony.

Visitors who enter the College pass bronze statues of General William Booth, founder of the Salvation Army in 1865, and his wife Catherine. The General's ambition was to found an 'International University of Humanity', which unfortunately he had been unable to do by the time of his death in 1912. The First World War delayed plans to build one as his memorial.

In 1921 the Salvation Army were looking for a site in South London. They chose the present site, rather than another possible one on Denmark Hill facing Herne Hill Congregational church because that site was not prominent enough. Sir Giles Gilbert Scott was chosen to be the college's architect. He later designed Waterloo Bridge and the present Liverpool Anglican Cathedral as well as Battersea and Bankside Power Stations. He also designed Britain's traditional red telephone box and was the architect for the rebuilding of the House of Commons after the Second World War. Scott stressed the importance of greenery and undertook to preserve as many mature trees as possible.

Alleyn's School

Alleyn's School in Townley Road dates from 1887 when it was built to house the Lower College of God's Gift. Townley Road was especially made in order to give ample access from Lordship Lane. The road took its name from Margaret Townley, the mother of Edward Alleyn, founder of Dulwich College.

The new school contained sixteen classrooms, offices, kitchens and servants' quarters but it had 'no gym and the field was a wilderness where the pheasant waged incessant war on the mangel-wurzel'.

A path, wide enough to take a horse and cart, was cut from Dulwich Village to Alleyn's to enable easy access. This path was called 'Smith's Walk' and named after the headmaster the Revd J.H. Smith; it finished up opposite the front door of the school.

During the First World War 264 Old Boys were killed. They are remembered by the school organ above the platform in the Great Hall, which was installed in their memory.

In 1920 R.B. Henderson, who had been Master at Rugby School, became headmaster. He revolutionised ideas within the school. He once said, 'it will be boys you will teach here, not subjects'. Parents were told that the whole waking time of the boy belonged to the school.

In 1975 a major change of direction came when the first girls entered the school in the sixth form. The following year the school became co-educational with a first year intake of thirty girls. Various new buildings have been added to the school in recent years.

Alleyn's The Coeducational School was written by Arthur R. Chandler, the school's Honorary Archivist.

Alleyn's School, *c.* 1905.

James Allen's Girls' School.   Dulwich.

James Allen's Girls' School, Dulwich, *c.* 1905.

James Allen's Girls' School

James Allen's Girls' School in East Dulwich Grove is thought to be the oldest girls' school in London. It was founded in 1741 when James Allen, Master of Alleyn's College of God's Gift at Dulwich, gave some property in Kensington to endow his new school. He stipulated that the profits be applied 'towards finding a school mistress or mistresses to be resident in Dulwich for the instructing and teaching such and so many poor boys to read and so many poor girls to read and sew...' The school started in two rooms in the Bricklayers Arms, later called The French Horn, in Dulwich Village.

In 1857, an Act of Parliament passed to reorganize Alleyn's College of God's Gift also decreed that what was then called the Dulwich Free School should educate girls only. The school moved to new premises further along the village in 1866; the buildings are still used by Dulwich Hamlet School. The school became known as James Allen's Girls' School in 1878 and moved to its present site in 1886.

Botany Gardens were created in the school grounds soon after Dr Lilian Clarke joined the staff in 1896. It was the first such experiment by a school in this country. A further pioneering step was taken in 1902 when the country's first school laboratory equipped solely for botanical study was established.

Composer Gustav Holst began teaching at JAGS in 1904. The Prissian Theatre, named after former headmistress Iris Prissian, was opened by Jonathan Miller in 1983. JAGS was the first girls' school in the country with its own purpose-built theatre.

A well-illustrated history of the school *To Read and Sew... James Allen's Girls' School 1741-1991* was written by Brian Green.

Peckham's Original Library

The Livesey Museum for children in the Old Kent Road was originally Peckham's first library and was opened on 18 October 1890. This was a gift from George Livesey, chairman of the South Metropolitan Gas Company, to Camberwell Vestry which ran local affairs until Camberwell Borough Council began its work in 1900.

The library was replaced by North Peckham Library in 1966. The Victorian building was reopened as the Livesey Museum by the poet Sir John Betjeman on 30 March 1974. A statue of George Livesey, which used to be in the grounds of the gasworks opposite the museum, is in the courtyard as are other historical exhibits. These include a quarter-size model of Edgington's shopfront which was presented to Southwark Council after the shop was removed in 1967 to make way for the Bricklayer's Arms flyover. The firm had been founded in 1805 and specialised in tent, rope and sail making. The company made the 'flags' of the rigging for Nelson's flagship.

Newington Tollgate is also in the Livesey Museum courtyard. It was originally situated on Newington Causeway. The Newington Turnpike was set up by Act of Parliament in 1718 and was abolished with other tollgates in 1865.

Half the lower jawbone of a whale was excavated from Surrey Commercial Docks in 1979 and loaned to the museum. During the eighteenth century, Greenland Dock was important in the Arctic whaling trade. Whale jaws and blubber were brought back to the dock for oil extraction. Another exhibit is a bell from St Alban's School, Walworth Road, cast in 1856; it was rung to announce the start of the morning and afternoon school sessions.

Christ Church and the public library, Old Kent Road, before the Second World War.

Nunhead Library, 1896.

Nunhead Library

The foundation stone for Nunhead Library was laid on 11 April 1896 by John Passmore Edwards, editor, philanthropist and donor of the library. He was first met at the Vestry Hall in Peckham Road (where Southwark Town Hall is today) by Matthew Wallace, chairman of Camberwell Vestry, Mr F.G. Banbury MP and a large number of other people. After some complimentary speeches, a procession consisting largely of carriages was formed which proceeded to Nunhead Green. There was a plentiful display of bunting at several points and thousands of people turned out to line the streets. On the library site a large marquee had been erected in which the speeches were delivered.

Mr Edwards helped to lay the memorial stone with a silver trowel which bore the motto, 'Good deeds live on when the doers are no more'.

The architect who designed the library in late Tudor style was Mr Robert P. Whellock who also designed what today is the Livesey Museum. The library was opened on 1 December 1896. The ceremony should have been performed by Lady Burne-Jones but as she was ill her place was taken by Mrs Wallace, wife of Matthew Wallace. In her speech she said that people should show their appreciation for Mr Edwards' gift by making it a 'measureless source of instruction in ages to come'.

The library had a news room with all the London morning papers as well as the illustrated weekly papers. It also had a magazine room and a lending library containing over 6,000 volumes with space for an additional 7,000 books.

Dulwich Library

Actor Sir Henry Irving laid the foundation stone of Dulwich Library which was opened on 24 November 1897 by the Lord Chancellor, Lord Halsbury. He is famous for presiding over the production of the complete digest of *Laws of England* which are regularly updated and found in many libraries.

The *South London Press* reported the opening of the library saying it would 'serve a very large and growing neighbourhood' and this 'beautiful library has cost £5,800 of which sum Mr Passmore Edwards generously pays £5,000'. Camberwell Vestry, the forerunner of Camberwell Borough Council, paid the remaining £800 and laid out the ground around the library as a public garden.

Mr John Passmore Edwards was a philanthropist who donated his money to enable around seventy free libraries (including Nunhead), hospitals and convalescent homes to be built in the United Kingdom.

The site for Dulwich Library was given by the Estates' Governors of Alleyn's College of God's Gift. The architect was R.P. Whellock.

On 9 September 1940 a bomb landed on the north-west corner of Dulwich Library. After the Second World War an extension was built which included the hall for public meetings. This was opened by the Mayor of Camberwell, Alderman J.F.W. Lucas, on 25 September 1954.

Dulwich Library, c. 1940.

St George's Library, 1977.

St George's Library

The public library movement received a boost over a century ago when the foundation stone for St George's Library in Borough Road was laid in December 1897 by Mr Passmore Edwards. He was principally responsible for enabling the library to be built.

The first suggestion for a public library in St George's Parish came from Mr Edwards in a letter to the press in which he offered to build the library on condition that the parish adopted the Public Libraries Act 1892 and acquired a site. This Act of Parliament enabled all local government units, except counties, to become library authorities.

An organization was established for testing the feelings of parishioners. In March 1896 a poll of the parish was taken, and the Public Libraries Acts were adopted by a majority of 1,814. The Vestry, which ran local affairs until Southwark Borough Council was set up in 1900, proceeded to appoint commissioners. After considerable difficulties, they purchased a suitable leasehold site in Borough Road for £500. The freehold was purchased for £4,500. The library cost £12,556 to build and furnish to which total Mr Passmore Edwards donated £5,000.

Though it is no longer a library, the building can still be seen in Borough Road close to St George's Circus. The building has a basement and two floors. Originally the ground floor was used for news rooms, lending library, ladies' rooms and boys' room (as a nineteenth century newspaper described the women's and boys' toilets). A reference library was on the first floor, with a book store attached, a committee room, and part of the librarian's residence. The library was opened on 8 February 1899 by the Rt Hon. James Bryce MP. A picture of a carving on the library is included in *Visions of Southwark* by Peter Marcan.

34

Three

Health

Guy's Hospital

The hospital founded by Thomas Guy opened in 1726. Thomas was a very successful publisher and printer who made an enormous fortune in South Seas stock; he was also MP for Tamworth and a sheriff of the City of London. Thomas Guy died when he was eighty years old, just before the first patients were admitted to his hospital which contained 100 beds. In its early days there were 51 employees whose annual salaries, including those for the butler and his horse, amounted to £1,348 18s 8d. In 1735 a man was paid £20 for killing bed bugs!

In 1738/39 an east wing, designed by James Steer, was added and in 1744 a lunatic house was built with twenty beds. The west wing was added by Richard Jupp between 1774 and 1780. In 1780 cold, hot and vapour baths were installed. In 1799 Guy's Hospital became the first hospital in London to appoint a dental surgeon.

The buildings have changed much since the original hospital was built; Guy's suffered greatly from bombing in the Second World War. In 1961 the eleven-storey New Guy's House was opened and followed in 1975 by the thirty-storey Guy's Tower. Guy's has beds for 410 patients and is one of the great teaching hospitals in the world.

Thomas Guy was reburied in 1780 in the chapel under a fine tomb and statue by John Bacon.

Statue of Thomas Guy in the hospital grounds, c. 1920.

Maudsley Hospital, *c*. 1950.

The Maudsley

The Maudsley Hospital was named after Dr Henry Maudsley who was an eminent doctor in the field of mental illness. He donated to the London County Council a large sum of money for the establishment of a small hospital with research facilities.

The Maudsley Hospital opened in 1923 and initially treated patients who were willing to attend on a voluntary basis. It occupies a site in Camberwell next to the railway and across the road from King's College Hospital. Several Georgian residences continue to coexist on the campus with the main administration building which was decorated with white stone and columns. It was sometimes described as 'Wrenaissance' and is reminiscent of Hampton Court.

The wards behind were plain and functional in red brick. The hospital was extended several times before the Second World War. The medical school was taken over by the University of London just prior to the hospital amalgamating with Bethlem Hospital at Beckenham in 1948; it was renamed the Institute of Psychiatry. The two hospitals and the Institute offically became known as The Bethlem and Maudsley NHS Trust in 1994.

The Maudsley started with only a few single rooms. The sleeping accommodation was planned more like the open wards of general hospitals, with beds against the wall. On the verandahs eight or more beds could also be accommodated. With the rebuilding of the hospital in recent years, the trend to dormitories was reversed with a return to individual sleeping spaces.

The story of the Maudsley Hospital is told in *Scenes from Bedlam: A History of Caring for the Mentally Disordered at Bethlem Royal Hospital and the Maudsley* by David Russell.

St Olave's

Actor Sir Michael Caine was born at St Olave's Hospital which grew out of the infirmary of Rotherhithe Workhouse. This was run by the St Olave's Poor Law Union in the late nineteenth century.

The Poor Law in England went back to the time of Queen Elizabeth I, but the parish of Rotherhithe did not have a workhouse until the late 1720s. The minutes of the organization which ran local affairs, Rotherhithe Vestry, include a proposal of 29 April 1722 to establish a workhouse. However, no further action was taken until 1728. Then a workhouse was built in Lower Road, opposite what is now the junction with Neptune Street. Life inside the workhouse was far from pleasant. In 1835 four female inmates were threatened with transportation to what is now Tasmania off the coast of Australia due to bad conduct.

The workhouse was under the control of the Rotherhithe Board of Guardians from 1839 until 1869 when it became part of St Olave's Union which took its name from St Olave's church near London Bridge. Poor Law Unions were encouraged by the Poor Law Amendment Act 1834 as it was more economical to join parishes together for providing assistance to poor people.

St Olave's Union ran the Poor Law in Rotherhithe from 1869 until 1930. During that time the workhouse was closed in 1884 but the infirmary continued to exist. In 1904 the St Olave's Union was renamed the Bermondsey Union so its hospital became the Bermondsey Infirmary. The name was changed to St Olave's Hospital in 1930 when the London County Council started to run it. The hospital closed in 1984.

Bermondsey Infirmary, 1925.

The New Bethlem Hospital as it appeared when it opened in 1815. This picture is included in *Bethlem Hospital 1247-1997: A Pictorial Record* by Patricia Allderidge.

Bethlem Hospital

The Imperial War Museum is housed in part of the former Bethlem Hospital. When the line of the road was altered in the 1830s the governors acquired more land at the front, enabling them to move the wall and lay out ornamental gardens with the distinctive oval lawn which still exists today.

The hospital was founded in 1247 as the Priory of St Mary of Bethlehem. The original site lies beneath Liverpool Street station. From there it moved to Moorfields and then to St George's Fields.

In two independent blocks at the back of Bethlem Hospital, the new State Criminal Lunatic Asylum was housed. It remained there from 1816 until it was replaced by a new institution at Broadmoor in Berkshire in 1864.

Improvements were made in Bethlem Hospital in the approach to the mentally ill patients from 1852 under the leadership of the young resident physician Dr (later Sir) Charles Hood, and the steward George Henry Haydon. The wards were more comfortably furnished. Birds, flowers, books, pictures and music were introduced. Occupation and recreation were provided both inside and outside the hospital walls.

Bethlem Hospital, known as Bedlam, remained at St George's Fields until 1930 when the patients were transferred to a new hospital at Beckenham.

The Royal Eye Hospital

The hospital was founded in 1857 by John Zachariah Laurence in premises which were houses built in 1821-1825 for Mary Johnson, proprietor of the 'Equestrian Coffee House'. It was first known as the South London Opthalmic Hospital and was situated at St George's Circus.

The hospital was under the patronage of HM King George of Hanover, HRH The Duke of Cambridge and HRH The Crown Princess of Prussia (who became HIM The Empress Frederick of Germany).

The number of patients rose from 446 in 1859 to 6,639 in 1890 so a new hospital was needed. The foundation stone of the new building was laid on 24 July 1890 by HRH The Prince of Wales, patron of the hospital.

The new hospital, called The Royal Eye Hospital or The Royal South London Ophthalmic Hospital, was opened on an extended site on 15 December 1892 by HRH The Duke of York. It was the only charity of its kind in London south of the Thames, and served a population of 1,600,000, whereas there were four similar charities in north London.

The new hospital had forty beds but fourteen were later closed through lack of funds. The building stood on sand and had no drain under it. It was open on the north, south, west and east. Every corner was rounded for cleanliness and for the convenience of those patients who were temporarily blindfolded.

The hospital was incorporated into the National Health Service in 1948 and eventually came under the control of St Thomas's Hospital. It closed in 1984. Whilst the hospital was being demolished in 1994 it collapsed on to a busy road; fortunately no one was hurt in the accident. The site is now occupied by a hostel for over 600 South Bank University students.

The Royal South London Ophthalmic Hospital, 1897.

What is now Dulwich Hospital, *c*. 1905.

Dulwich Hospital

The future of Dulwich Hospital is uncertain but there is no doubt about its past because the history was outlined in a brochure to mark the opening of the Operating Theatre Suite in 1958.

At the close of the nineteenth century, Charles Booth in his monumental work *Life and Labour of the People in London* estimated that 'after deducting loafers and criminals, 29.8% of the people are in perpetual poverty owing to the family earnings being less than 21s per week.' From 1850 onwards the problem of pauperism had become increasingly poignant in the numerous parishes of South London, and the Poor Law Unions found it hard to find accommodation for sick poor people.

In 1871 this was especially the situation in the St Saviour's Union, Surrey, covering the parishes of Christ Church, Blackfriars, St George the Martyr, Southwark, St Mary, Newington, and St Saviour which later became the Metropolitan Borough of Southwark.

Newington Workhouse in 1871 was grossly overcrowded with poor and sick people so the Poor Law Authority was forced into action to find a remedy. In that year it was decided to erect an infirmary building outside the bounds of the Union, in the breezy, unspoilt countryside near Peckham Rye Common. In January 1872 the idea was abandoned in favour of an enlargement of Newington Workhouse. Nine years then elapsed, by which time the matter of accommodation for sick poor people had become yet more urgent. The site, adjoining Champion Hill station (later renamed East Dulwich station), and covering an area of over 6 acres, was acquired for £14,000.

The projected new infirmary aroused much opposition in Camberwell and East Dulwich. Despite the outcry, the St Saviour's Union proceeded with its plans and the opening ceremony was held on 13 April 1887.

The Peckham Experiment

A famous health experiment was started at No. 142 Queen's Road, Peckham, in 1926. As the project developed, a purpose-built centre was opened in St Mary's Road in 1935. The Peckham Pioneer Health Centre building still exists and has been converted for residential use.

The notable Peckham Experiment, as it was called, was begun by Dr George Scott Williamson and Dr Innes Pearse. The world-famous investigation into the nature and cultivation of health continued until 1950.

In *The King's England: London* Arthur Mee wrote: 'One of the most interesting of all Peckham's buildings is its remarkable Health Centre. It is a great club house for the families of Peckham, where they find every encouragement known to science to be healthy and happy, and wise. Here they may dance, fence, play games, enjoy physical exercises and swim in a beautiful blue-green bath. There is a children's bathing pool with a playground, a library, a cafeteria, a kitchen, a hall and a running-track. In setting up this great Health Centre Peckham has set a fine example to the densely peopled areas of our great cities. The West End of London has nothing to equal it.'

Britain's first healthy living centre, the Peckham Pulse, has drawn inspiration and ideas from the Peckham Pioneer Health Centre. Various books have been written about this unusual health centre including *The Peckham Experiment* by Innes H. Pearse and Lucy H. Crocker, *The Quality of Life* by Innes H. Pearse and *Being Me and Also Us* by Alison Stallibrass.

Peckham's famous Health Centre, *c.* 1938.

Bermondsey Spa, *c*. 1790.

Bermondsey Spa

Spa Road is a reminder of Bermondsey Spa which was situated at the corner of what are now Rouel Road and Spa Road. Bermondsey Spa was created by artist Thomas Keyse (1722-1800). After buying a public house in Bermondsey called the Waterman's Arms in around 1765, he saw the possibility of cashing in on the then current fashion for health as well as entertainments at spas, wells, watering places and seaside resorts. He converted some open fields at the rear of the tavern into pleasure gardens. For around thirty years Thomas Keyse maintained a tea garden, musical entertainment, firework and other displays. He also had an art gallery for his own paintings – all on the strength of a spring which was discovered in the grounds! This enabled him to give his creation the rather grandiose title of 'spa'.

It was actually referred to in *Old London's spas, baths and wells* as a 'spurious spa', together with a number in the City, where the water, reputedly of a somewhat muddy appearance, had little or no attraction for the visitors. On the other hand, some health seekers were persuaded into partaking.

In an 1883 book, *History of Bermondsey*, W. Lees Bell wrote: 'Another circumstance helped to make Bermondsey fashionable: certain physicians took to prescribing Bermondsey Water and an airing in the carriage through the streets and roads of Bermondsey to inhale the odour of the tan, which hath valuable tonic properties'. There were various tanning factories in the area in those days.

The spa continued for five years after Thomas Keyse died and then all his paintings were sold by auction. *Thomas Keyse and the Bermondsey Spa* by Frank Keyse gives more information.

Evelina Children's Hospital

Founded in Southwark in 1869, the hospital amalgamated with Guy's Children's Department in 1947 and they entered the National Health Service a year later as combined teaching hospitals. After the hospital in Southwark Bridge Road closed in 1975, a new Evelina Children's Department opened in the thirty-storey Guy's Tower.

The hospital began as a result of a tragedy in the nineteenth century. Baron Ferdinand de Rothschild, a member of the Vienna branch of the Rothschild family, longed to live in England, '... the land of my dreams', as he called it. His father did not object and so at the age of twenty-one he left Vienna to settle in London. From there he went up to Cambridge with his friend, Edward, Prince of Wales. In 1865 he married his cousin Evelina, daughter of Lionel, his mother's brother. Sadly, in 1866 Baroness Evelina went into labour prematurely following a railway accident. Her physician obstetrician, Dr Arthur Farre, was present but tragically both mother and child died.

Baron de Rothschild founded the Evelina Children's Hospital in their memory. It was designed by Dr Farre and its doors opened in 1869. Dr Farre was the first chairman of its committee of management and the hospital's consultant physician.

The Evelina Hospital was one of the pioneers of unlimited visiting. It was a forerunner in other ways too. Cubicles in every ward for mothers to stay beside their children were among the first to be built in this country. In 1948 it became the first hospital to employ its own teaching staff.

The former Evelina Hospital, 1977.

St Francis Hospital, 1986.

Constance Road Infirmary

St Francis Hospital in East Dulwich was originally the Constance Road Workhouse built for the Camberwell Board of Guardians. The foundation stone was laid on 21 July 1892. The workhouse opened in 1895 and had accommodation for 898 inmates. It became the Constance Road Infirmary and specialised in caring for the 'deserving poor', mentally ill and handicapped people, elderly people and unmarried mothers.

This continued until 1930 when the infirmary came under the control of the London County Council and started to care for chronically sick people. It was renamed St Francis Hospital in 1936.

During the Second World War it was used as a reception centre for bombed-out families. At this time the children's block was destroyed by bombing. In 1948 the hospital was taken over by the National Health Service and was under the administrative control of the Camberwell Hospital Management Committee.

In April 1966 St Francis Hospital formally became part of King's College Hospital Group and was designated as a teaching unit. Following the reorganization of the NHS it became part of Camberwell Health Authority in 1974. The hospital was renamed Dulwich Hospital in 1984 and was identified as Dulwich North. It then closed in 1991 and St Francis Place now occupies the site.

St Giles's Hospital

St Giles's Hospital owed its origin to an institution founded under the Poor Law of 1601. On 26 December 1726 the Vestry of St Giles', Camberwell, unanimously resolved 'that a workhouse shall be built for lodging and employing the poor in work'. After many subsequent meetings at which certain opposition was met, it was finally 'unanimously agreed' on 7 March 1727 'that Mr William Norman shall build the workhouse... at the price of £365' and for that purpose the churchwardens and overseers borrowed £400.

In 1728 'before the furnishing and compleating' of the structure, the expenses had mounted to £500, for which bonds were signed, and on 31 June 1731 William Row was appointed beadle of the parish and master of the new workhouse. This stood on the west corner of Workhouse Lane, later to be known as Havil Street, at its junction with Peckham Road.

By 1815, after alterations and enlargements, the growth of population and pauperism made a new building necessary and the old workhouse was demolished. A new, larger workhouse was erected at the rear of the old site, flanking Havil Street, and this was added to from 1873 by the Camberwell Board of Guardians who built an infirmary. A circular ward block, which has been preserved, was added in 1888-1889. Four more ward blocks were provided in 1903.

The hospital was transferred to the London County Council in 1930. A new operating theatre and reception were provided four years later. The Princess of Wales visited the Drug Dependency Unit of St Giles's Hospital in 1985.

Much of the original St Giles's Hospital building still exists even though Camberwell Health Authority voted in 1983 to close most of the facilities.

St Giles's Hospital, c. 1900.

The nineteenth-century operating theatre discovered in 1956.

How It Used to be Done

The roof garret of the eighteenth century church of St Thomas's, near London Bridge, contains a reconstruction of an old operating theatre. It dates from 1821 and was part of St Thomas's Hospital before it closed in 1862 and moved to Lambeth. The timber garret was also used by the apothecary for the storage and curing of herbs to be used in the hospital medicines.

The theatre witnessed the advent of anaesthesia in 1846 and was closed three years before Lister began his experiment in antiseptic surgery. Florence Nightingale founded her School of Nursing at the old hospital in 1860 and advised on the hospital's subsequent move.

After St Thomas's Hospital moved, the operating theatre remained hidden and largely forgotten until, in 1956, its site within the roof space of the church was again identified. It was this seclusion in the roof space of the church, which continued as a parish church until 1898 and subsequently became the Chapter House for Southwark Cathedral, that was responsible for its preservation while all other early nineteenth century operating theatres were either destroyed or modernized.

The historic building in St Thomas's Street is not only unique but remarkable due to its dramatic setting. The site, together with the museum collection of medical instruments and herbal medicines, is a reminder of the major advances in medical treatment over the past 150 years.

The story of how the old operating theatre was discovered is told in the Museum Guide.

Four

Housing

The Legacy of Charles Hopton

Hopton's Almshouses, familiar to Charles Dickens, in Hopton Street were opened in 1752. Very little is known about the founder of these almshouses; Charles Hopton died on 6 March 1730 aged seventy-six and was buried in Broadway Chapel, Westminster. The chapel no longer exists but the churchyard can be seen opposite New Scotland Yard.

Five days before Charles died he made a will, leaving a large sum of money. The interest was paid to his sister Elizabeth for life. After she died in 1739, the remaining money was used to build twenty-six almshouses for 'poor decayed' men who had been resident householders in the parish of Christ Church, Southwark. In addition, each resident received £6 a year and one chaldron (32 bushels) of coal.

The estate was administered by the rector and churchwardens of the parish together with other trustees. Some of the earliest residents were gardeners, artisans, watermen and fishermen.

An old and heavy calf-bound volume still exists containing, in spidery copper-plate writing with flourishing capitals and in faded brown ink on yellowed paper, the history, rules and accounts of the almhouses in the eighteenth century. Some of the old rules are particularly interesting. There were fines for 'resorting to alehouses', 6d being the fine for the first offence, 1s for the second, and 2s for the third. The use of 'railing, bitter or uncharitable speech' by any one pensioner to another, or by any pensioner's wife to another, was also penalised at the same rate. Swearing, after the first two offences, was slightly more expensive.

Hopton's Almshouses, 1910.

An engraving of Winchester Palace showing damage by fire in 1814.

Winchester Palace

Remains of Winchester Palace can still be seen in Clink Street, including the stone tracery of a fourteenth-century rose window. The Palace was the London residence of the Bishops of Winchester from the 1140s until 1626.

In the mid-twelfth century Henry de Blois, Bishop of Winchester, acquired land on the river-front for a London residence because of 'the many inconveniences and losses sustained through the lack of a house of our own when called to London on royal or other business'.

Winchester Square was once the inner courtyard of the palace. A fire destroyed the hall of the palace on 28 August 1814; most of the walls were subsequently demolished.

Nearby Park Street is a reminder of the Bishop of Winchester's park, or estate, which stretched from the priory walls in what is now Cathedral Street to Gravel Lane, now called Great Suffolk Street. A document described it as 'all the episcopal pastures belonging to the bishop's manor in Southwark'. There were sheep and cows, ponds to supply the bishop's household with fish, a granary for storing corn and a mill. From river stairs at the end of Stoney Street the bishop was able to go by boat to the King's court at Westminster. The last bishop to live at Winchester Palace was Lancelot Andrewes who died in 1626.

During the Civil War, Winchester Palace was used by Parliament as a prison for their Royalist captives. It was later divided up and used for housing and industry until most of it was destroyed by the fire in 1814.

The Bessemer Estate

Bessemer Grange School stands on what was the lake within the grounds of Sir Henry Bessemer's estate on Denmark Hill. When he died in 1898, it covered forty acres and included two imposing houses, a model farm, underground caverns, and an observatory housing the second largest telescope in the world.

Sir Henry was a prolific Victorian inventor and engineer. During his lifetime he took out 144 patents but he is best remembered as the inventor of the Bessemer Converter; this meant that it was possible to mass produce steel in place of iron. Industry was revolutionised and the production of steel drove many countries forward. In the USA a number of towns were named after him.

In 1947 both houses were demolished to make way for an estate of around 600 homes. Bessemer House was designed by Charles Barry, son of the architect of the Houses of Parliament. Adjacent to it was Bessemer Grange built for Sir Henry's daughter.

W.H. Blanch wrote about the model farm in *Ye Parish of Camerwell*, published in 1875, saying: '... whether it has ever been conducted as an experimental one to test any particular system of agriculture is doubtful: there are two cottages erected on the land, which are occupied by undergardeners'. The farm terminated at the railway cutting.

When the lease expired on the model farm, it was conveyed to James Allen's Girls' School for a nominal sum. In the 1960s the near-derelict model farm was replaced by a new pavilion which was later converted into the Music School.

Bessemer House and Lake, *c.* 1910.

Basing Manor House, 1883.

Basing Manor

Basing Manor House used to stand in the Surrey village of Peckham until it was demolished in 1883. It included beautiful specimens of oak panelling and antique carving. The manor existed in the fourteenth century.

Melon Road off Peckham High Street is a reminder that Sir Thomas Gardiner (died 1632), who lived at Basing Manor House, sent some melons to King Charles I after the King had visited him and sent him 'a fat venison in melon time'. Sir Thomas was Lord of the Manor and one of the Justices of the Peace for Surrey.

The Manor House School began using the quaint old Basing Manor House in 1854. Attached to the school were $2\frac{1}{2}$ acres of land used as a recreation ground by the female pupils. After the school was demolished, a horse tram depot was built on the site; this was later used for electric trams. Rye Lane Depot, in what today is Bellenden Road, had space for 106 trams in 1909.

The depot was taken over by the military authorities during the First World War and was returned to the London County Council in 1919. It was used for permanent way storage and subsequently by London Transport as a garage for motor vehicles other than buses. A bus garage was built on the site in 1952. In the 1960s the Department of Employment took over the garage for use as a repair workshop for buses until 1986. The garage was later used as a factory producing Comply plasterboard products.

The Concrete House

The house at No. 549 Lordship Lane, now an important listed building, is in a derelict state. Southwark Council has refused permission for it to be demolished and wants it to be restored. The house was built in 1873 by Charles Drake of the Patent Concrete Building Company. Although the original building application has not survived, the application for the laying of drainage pipes, dated 11 February 1873, still exists and has Charles Drake's signature on it.

The block plan and drainage layout of the building, which accompanied the application, corresponds exactly with the present structure. The application was approved by the Camberwell Vestry Surveyor on 25 February 1873.

The earliest record of the occupation of No. 549 Lordship Lane survives in the 1881 census. The house was called The Ferns and was occupied by Robert Fenn Carter, a fifty-six-year-old linen merchant from Ireland. Mr Carter lived with his wife Bessie, daughters Lizzie and Murilla, Jane Spicer, housemaid, and Emma Claydon, cook. Charles Drake was a speculative builder and it is probable that he sold the house to Mr Carter soon after it was built.

In 1867 Charles Drake patented his own method for building with concrete. Drake used sheet iron panels instead of timber shuttering. The house in Lordship Lane is a rare example of a nineteenth century concrete house. There is no other known property of this type and of the same architectural style in England today.

Number 549 Lordship Lane, East Dulwich, in 1983, before this nineteenth-century concrete house was allowed to deteriorate.

The Prince of Wales, the future King Edward VII, unveiled this marble statue of his late father, Prince Albert, in 1864.

The Licensed Victuallers Asylum

Caroline Gardens in Asylum Road, Peckham, was named after Caroline Sophie Secker who was a resident in what was then known as the Licensed Victuallers Asylum. She was the widow of Sergeant James Secker of the Marines who served with Horatio Nelson at the Battle of Trafalgar in 1805. Mrs Secker died in the Asylum in 1845.

In 1827 the Licensed Victuallers purchased land on which to build an asylum to provide homes for retired members of the trade. The first stone was laid on 29 May 1828 by HRH the Duke of Sussex, the sixth son of George III. The building contract was for 43 houses but in 1831 a new wing with 29 houses was begun due to large demand. Two years later the north wing, comprising a further 29 houses, was started. Then in 1849 a new part called 'The Ladies' Wing', comprising 16 houses, was added. The first stone was laid by HRH Prince Albert, consort to Queen Victoria.

The following year an additional 7 houses as well as a chapel, boardroom and spacious court-room were added to the complex. In 1858, 15 more houses were built; these were designated the Albert Wing as Prince Albert again officiated. In the following year 6 extra houses were erected, with a further 13 in 1862.

In 1866 HRH the Duke of Edinburgh, fourth child of Queen Victoria, laid the foundation of the 'Smalley' wing, in the presence of the Lord Mayor and sheriffs. The name of the new wing commemorated the founder, William Smalley, secretary to the Incorporated Society of Licensed Victuallers.

By the 1870s the asylum consisted of 170 units of accommodation; 205 residents were provided with shelter, financial help, coal, medicine and medical advice. In 1959, when the Licensed Victuallers decided to move their retired people to new homes at Denham in Buckinghamshire, the property was acquired by Camberwell Borough Council which renamed the asylum Caroline Gardens. The statue of Prince Albert was moved to Denham in 1960.

Workhouses

The former 'Spike' in Peckham's Gordon Road, which opened as a workhouse in 1879, was converted into flats in the 1990s by a housing association. It was built in the grounds of Nazareth House because the parish of Camberwell had many poor people so a new workhouse was needed.

Nazareth House stood where Cross Close is today. It was built as a convent and had a large cross at the top of the building. The convent was built in a quiet spot when Peckham was still part of Surrey. The nuns moved out when the railway was built because it destroyed the privacy and quietness of the grounds.

In the early 1870s, 110 aged and infirm male paupers lived in Nazareth House. The inmates, many of whom had been tradesmen in the parish, engaged in various industrial pursuits. The four acres of grounds were used by pigs and poultry as well as for growing potatoes, parsnips, onions, carrots, rhubarb, lettuces and other produce. The inmates made a pony cart and Venetian blinds. Others acted as blacksmiths.

As the number of paupers in the parish of Camberwell increased, another workhouse was needed so a new one was built in the grounds of Nazareth House. This became known as The Spike. In return for a night's lodging, a tramp had to break a certain amount of stone into pieces small enough to go through a grille. One grille is preserved at the Livesey Museum in the Old Kent Road. There were times when The Spike housed over 1,000 men. It closed in 1985.

The 'Spike'.

Kingswood House, 1956.

Bovril Castle

Kingswood House in Dulwich may have been named after Edward King who was a tenant of Dulwich manor in 1535. William Vizard began to build Kingswood Lodge (later renamed Kingswood House) in 1811. He was a solicitor involved with one of the most sensational legal cases of his time – the divorce proceedings brought in the House of Lords by George IV against Queen Caroline in 1820. Vizard was the Queen's legal adviser.

Kingswood was acquired in the 1890s by John Lawson Johnston, who invented a beef extract which he called Bovril, so the house became known as 'Bovril Castle'. Johnston added the entrance, battlements and the north wing.

During the First World War, Kingswood was sub-let to Massey-Harris, a Canadian firm of tractor manufacturers for use as a hospital for Canadian troops. After the war it became a nurses' home for several months. In 1919 Kingswood was bought by Sir William Vestey who became Baron Vestey of Kingswood. It was being used as a recuperation centre for wounded troops and came to the notice of Lady Vestey when she was doing social work in connection with the soldiers housed there.

Kingswood was in a state of disrepair after the Second World War but was renovated and opened as a community centre and library in 1956.

Girdlers' Almshouses

The Girdlers' Company erected almhouses in Peckham and Nunhead in the nineteenth century, which are still in use today.

Beeston's in Consert Road were built in 1834. A Gothic water pump stands in the grounds and, although not in its original position, it is a reminder of how residents obtained water before piped supplies became available.

Palyn's Almshouses in Choumert Road, now called Girdlers' Cottages, were opened in 1852. As the name suggests, girdlers made girdles, or belts – and especially their associated metal-work. Girdles were often ornate, and were worn outside the tunic or gown. They might simply be to gather in the garment, but were also used to suspend the wallet, purse or side-arms.

The Worshipful Company of Girdlers erected almshouses in Albert (now Consort) Road to commemorate the good deeds of Cuthbert Beeston who was Master of the Company in 1570. In his will dated 5 July 1582, Beeston gave to the Girdlers' Company premises in the parish of St Olave, Southwark, on condition that they make annual payments out of the rents. He also directed that the residue of the rents should be used to provide loans for one year to the poorest members of the Company. The property gradually increased in value and was sold so the land could provide access to a new London Bridge. The money raised was used to build almshouses.

A drawing of the Nunhead almshouses is included in *A Historical Tour of Nunhead and Peckham Rye* by Ron Woollacott.

Attractive nineteenth-century almshouses, seen here in 1953.

Blackfriars Peabody Estate, Blackfriars Road, *c.* 1900.

George Peabody

Blackfriars Estate is one of various estates in Southwark built by the Peabody Trust. Most of the estate was completed in 1871 but modernization began in 1988; it now has Grade II listed status.

The Peabody Trust is a general charity for low-income Londoners which was set up nearly 140 years ago. It is now the capital's largest and longest established charitable housing trust with over 17,000 homes for rent across 24 boroughs. The Trust exists because of the generosity of George Peabody (1795-1869) who was born in Massachusetts. He made the beginning of his fortune in Baltimore during the city's rapid growth as a key port and centre of trade. In 1837 he moved to London where for the rest of his life he directed his empire from the financial capital of the Victorian world. Peabody amassed the money needed to push the American railroads westward and was a director of the company that laid the first transatlantic cables.

As a youth of seventeen, George Peabody joined as a volunteer soldier when the British fleet was advancing on Washington. Ironically, years after enlisting to fight the British in the war of 1812, he became an unofficial diplomatic eminence in London, fostering commercial relations and political goodwill between America and England.

In 1862 George Peabody founded the Peabody Donation Fund, providing £500,000 for 'the construction of such improved dwellings for the poor as may combine in the utmost possible degree the essentials of healthfulness, comfort, social enjoyment and economy' for Londoners. Queen Victoria acknowledged this as a gift 'wholly without parallel'.

When Peabody died, the carriages of the Queen and the Prince of Wales followed the hearse to Westminster Abbey where Prime Minister Gladstone was amongst the mourners.

In *George Peabody: A Biography* Franklin Parker recorded that on 11 July 1962 Queen Elizabeth, the Queen Mother, unveiled a plaque in honour of George Peabody on the Blackfriars Estate. Many Southwark residents benefit today from Peabody's important work.

56

Friendly Female Society

The World Garden in Chumleigh Gardens, a beautiful and unusual aspect of Burgess Park, was constructed adjacent to almshouses. These were originally erected by the Friendly Female Society in 1821.

The Society was founded in 1802 'for the relief of poor infirm aged widows and single women of good character who have seen better days'. The rules at first limited recipients of assistance to those living within five miles of St Paul's Cathedral, but this was extended to seven miles in 1891 and later to ten. The Society is notable for the fact that even from its beginnings it was run by an exclusively female committee (although the trustees appointed for its property in 1821 had to be men).

Queen Victoria was a patron of this charity. A plaque on the building used to read: 'The Friendly Female Asylum for aged persons who have seen better days. Erected and supported by voluntary contributions 1821'.

In 1871 the almshouses had forty-one residents. Today the Southwark Parks Ranger Service is based there as well as a Parks Visitor Centre. The multi-cultural garden close to the former almshouses has plants from all around the world.

Almshouses, 1969.

The estate of Belair, 1934.

Belair

Belair in Dulwich Village was built around 1785 for John Willes and was originally known as 'College Place'. The lease granted to John Willes was renewed in 1806 on condition that he undertook 'to underdrain the land between Dulwich Road (later named Gallery Road) and 'the Sheet of Water' (at the bottom) and 'that part of the Pasture Land which is Poachy and Wet'.

After John Willes died, the name of the property was changed to Belair by Charles Ranken, a solicitor of Lincoln's Inn, who moved into the house in 1829 and remained there until he died in 1858.

The next resident was Charles William Cookworthy Hutton who was a merchant in the City of London. He was a 'Berlin Wool Manufacturer and Wholesaler'. Berlin wool was very widely used by Victorian ladies until around 1880, and still exists today.

In the 1860s over ten acres of the grounds were sold by Dulwich College to the London, Chatham and Dover Railway, where the railway now runs. The last private owner of Belair was Sir Evan Spicer, who was a member of the London County Council; his lease began in 1893. At this time the house had forty-seven separate rooms and there was a farm which had cows, horses, chickens, pigs, ducks and other animals. After Sir Evan Spicer died in 1938, the property was sold by auction.

During the Second World War the house fell into decay. It was used as a store by Evan Cook & Co and the military occupied it for a time. Then in 1946 the Metropolitan Borough of Southwark took out a lease on the building and its grounds to be a 'green lung' for their residents.

Five
Parks and Open Spaces

Southwark Park

This park was in the parish of Rotherhithe but took its name from the parliamentary constituency of Southwark in which it was situated when it was opened in 1869. The town of Southwark lay well to the west, beyond Bermondsey. In 1921/22 the local Member of Parliament, John Lort Williams, tried to have the name changed to Rotherhithe Park but the London County Council rejected the idea.

Market gardens had covered the land which was bought by the Metropolitan Board of Works in order to make its first park. Most of the land was purchased from the Lord of the Manor of Rotherhithe, Sir William Maynard Gomm.

The lake was created in 1885 and extended in 1908. It was an extensive feature in the centre of the park and was far bigger than today's pond. Another big feature in the early part of the twentieth century was the cricket ground which was sited towards Hawkstone Road and was known as the Oval. The celebrated Victorian cricketer Robert Abel, who was born in Rotherhithe, learnt his skills as a member of the Southwark Park Cricket Club. He first played for Surrey in 1881. He was chosen as *Wisden's* cricketer of the year in 1890. He was a master batsman who made 357 not out against Somerset at the Oval in Kennington in 1899. Abel played his thirteenth and last test match – England *v.* Australia – in 1902. Failing eyesight forced 'The Guvnor', as this tiny Surrey player was known, to retire in 1904.

Southwark Park is currently being renovated.

Boating on the lake in Southwark Park.

Geraldine Mary Harmsworth Park, 1934.

Geraldine Mary Harmsworth Park

A Tibetan Peace Garden was created in Geraldine Mary Harmsworth Park. The Tibet Foundation commissioned the garden to fulfil their commitment to creating a better understanding between different cultures and to establish places of peace and harmony in the world. The garden was opened by His Holiness the Dalai Lama of Tibet on 13 May 1999.

The park itself was opened in 1934 by the chairman of the London County Council, Lord Snell. It was created in the grounds of the former Bethlem Hospital which moved to Monks Orchard, Beckenham. The land was purchased by newspaper proprietor Viscount Rothermere who presented it to the public as a permanent memorial to his mother, Geraldine Mary Harmsworth. It was subsequently agreed that the former hospital should be used by the Imperial War Museum which was then housed at South Kensington. A children's lido was opened in the park in 1938.

The park was created on land previously known as St George's Fields. These fields extended over a considerable part of Southwark, and originally formed part of a marshy tract of sparsely populated land reaching from Deptford to Lambeth.

Before they were enclosed, St George's Fields formed a favourite Sunday resort for Londoners. In *Herbal*, published in 1597, Gerald wrote: 'Of water violets I have not found such plenty in any one place as in the water ditches adjoining to Saint George his fielde, near London'.

In 1551 Edward VI granted several acres 'of meadow in divers parcels in St George's Fields' to the City Corporation in trust for the Bridge House. This grant included the site of the park.

Brunswick Park

Opened by the Mayor of Camberwell on 15 July 1907, Brunswick Park had previously been a private garden maintained by residents who lived in surrounding houses. A road which formerly divided the park into two portions was added to the park making it roughly four acres. Moves to acquire the land for the park took place fourteen years before it was opened. Many difficulties were encountered during the negotiations.

It is probable that the park formed a portion of the sixty-three acres of meadow land mentioned in *Domesday Book* as being attached to St Giles's church.

The *South London Press* reported the opening ceremony: 'Streamers and flags were abundantly in evidence, and the magnificent weather added to the pleasures of the occasion.' Brunswick Park was considered to be one of the prettiest open spaces in South London. In his speech during the opening ceremony, the Mayor of Camberwell, Cllr Lane Mitchell, expressed the hope that the park might give joy and comfort to many future generations, and that they would rise up and call those blessed who worked for the park's creation.

In 1937 two hard tennis courts and a children's playground were made. They were officially opened on 9 October by the Mayor of Camberwell, Cllr J. Clark. The new equipment provided was an all-metal slide, a plank swing, an Ocean Wave, a merry-go-round, and two swings which included four seats in each. A bubble drinking fountain was presented by the Metropolitan Drinking Fountain Association.

Brunswick Park, 1953.

Dulwich Park, *c.* 1905.

Dulwich Park

In 1885 the Estates Governors of Alleyn's College of God's Gift gave the old 'Five Fields' of Dulwich Court Farm, and other land, to be laid out by the Metropolitan Board of Works as a park. The old stone bridge still has the coat of arms of the 'M.B.W.' Dulwich Park was opened by Lord Rosebery in 1890 and since that time many things have remained unchanged; ducks swim on the Victorian lake and tea can still be enjoyed in the same tea-room. Lord Rosebery was the first chairman of the London County Council and one of the gates is named after him. Another gate is named after Queen Mary who visited the park every year to see the magnificent rhododendrons.

Lieutenant Colonel J.J. Sexby, Chief Officer of Parks for both the Metropolitan Board of Works and the London County Council, was responsible for its design. He wrote: 'The principal entrance is facing the old college chapel, hard by the famous picture gallery, and taking our stand here we obtain an excellent view across the park to the surrounding hills, dotted with graceful church spires. The Crystal Palace is within sight, only a mile distant, while closer at hand is Dulwich College School, hidden from view by the belts of giant trees which give the neighbourhood so rural an appearance.'

An article in *Gardeners Chronicle* in 1891 stated: 'The park provided for the public exactly what was wanted – wide lawns, old Oaks, cricket grounds, ample spaces for lawn tennis and football, a delightful smooth road for cyclists, and a lounge with seats for young couples who have negotiations to carry on.'

Peckham Rye Park

Whalebone arches were a popular feature in Peckham Rye Park. Their origin remained a mystery until *Peckham Rye Park 1894-1994* was published to mark the park's centenary. After reading the book a lady wrote a letter to *Peckham Society News* saying that the arches were provided by her great grandfather who lived in Homestall Road and the whalebone arches were a feature of his garden. They had probably been acquired by a relative who had been in the whaling industry.

Peckham Rye Park was opened on Whit Monday, 14 May 1894. It was created on land that had been Homestall Farm. The reason the farm was converted into a park was that Peckham Rye Common was so crowded on Saturdays and Bank Holidays that there was concern about the safety of the people. It was decided that more space was needed for recreational activities.

On the day the park opened, there was a long procession of trade and temperance society bands and banners, marching all the way from Camberwell Vestry Hall (where Southwark Town Hall in Peckham Road is today). The streets through which the procession passed on its way to the park were gaily decorated and the footpaths on both sides were packed with people. About 100,000 adults and children were on the Rye and in the park during the day.

Whalebone arches, Peckham Rye Park.

A bombed site in Lynton Road where Paterson Park was created, 1950.

Paterson Park

Bermondsey's Paterson Park and the man it commemorates deserve to be more widely known. Paterson Park was opened in 1953 by Clem Attlee. The park was extended after the Bricklayers' Arms goods station was closed in 1981. The Bricklayers' Arms Nature Reserve can be reached from the park under a former railway bridge.

The park was named after Sir Alexander Henry Paterson (1884-1947), a notable prison reformer. After studying at Oxford University he worked among poor people in Bermondsey and wrote a moving account of his experience in *Across the Bridges*, published in 1911. He made his home in Bermondsey until his marriage and became an unpaid teacher in Riley Elementary School.

Once a year, for fourteen years, Alec cycled 200 miles from London to Dartmoor to visit a man who had killed his own newly wedded wife during a fit of temporary insanity. Alec Paterson undertook the supervision of boys released from Borstal institutions. In 1911 he became assistant director of the Central Association for the Aid of Discharged Prisoners. During the First World War he served with the Bermondsey battalion in France. He became a commissioner of prisons and Director of Convict Prisons in 1922. He brought the human touch into life behind bars; he sought prisoners' rehabilitation by abolishing practices destructive of self-respect by providing recreational and educational facilities and the introduction of open prisons. In Borstal institutions he replaced enforced obedience with educational methods based on a house system designed to invite co-operation and inculcate new standards.

Alec Paterson also advised on penal administration in Burma, Ceylon, the West Indies, East and West Africa, Malta and Gibraltar, and was knighted in 1947.

64

Houses were demolished to make way for a Peabody Estate. In the background is Greencoat School.

Camberwell Green

Camberwell Fair was held every year on Camberwell Green. In the Middle Ages it lasted for three weeks and gave local residents the opportunity to buy goods they could not produce on their own land. Later the fair lasted for only three days and was simply a time for entertainment. However, as there was a great deal of disturbance and annoyance to the residents, there was agitation for the fair to end and it was abolished in 1855.

A few energetic individuals raised a subscription among the 'local gentry' for the purpose of purchasing the exclusive rights of holding the fair from the then Lords of the Manor, Sir William Bowyer Smyth and Sir Thomas Dyer. In 1856, the Lords of the Manor sold the rights of the fair for £1,250 to William Wild, Frank Clarke Hills, Charles Milhouse and Richard Dawes – and also conveyed the green to them. Then on 13 September 1857 these men sold Camberwell Green to the Vestry of the Parish of St Giles, Camberwell, which ran local affairs before Camberwell Borough Council was set up in 1900.

Camberwell Green is also famous in another way – it had inspired Mendelssohn to write his *Spring Song*. The original title was *Camberwell Green* and the composer wrote it when he was staying in 1842 at Denmark Hill with a German family who were relatives of his wife.

The Bandstand, Peckham Rye Common, c. 1910.

Peckham Rye Common

Victorian streets would have been built on Peckham Rye if local people had not fought in the 1860s to preserve this common land. To stop the lord of the manor, Sir William Bowyer Smyth, allowing buildings to be erected on the Rye, the manorial rights were purchased in 1868 by Camberwell Vestry, a forerunner of Southwark Council. Old minute books of Camberwell Vestry preserved in Southwark Local Studies Library show that in 1766 and 1789 there was concern about encroachments on Peckham Rye.

Various organizations made good use of the common in the nineteenth century. W.H. Blanch wrote in *Ye Parish of Camerwell* (1875): 'The more robust youth have a capital field for the exercise of outdoor sports on the fine open space of Peckham Rye, and therefore cricket-clubs and athletic societies flourish amongst us.'

However, great difficulty was experienced before 1869 in keeping order on Peckham Rye and in preventing it from becoming the site of a huge fair. In 1864, thirty-two vans of 'Wombwell's wild beasts' took up residence, and other invasions, more or less objectionable, were made from time to time.

A bandstand was transferred to the Rye in 1889 by the London County Council. It was one of a pair originally erected in the Royal Horticultural Society's Garden in Kensington in 1861. The other was moved to Southwark Park and a replica was erected on Clapham Common. The Peckham one was blown up after it had been partially destroyed by a land mine during the Second World War.

One Tree Hill

One Tree Hill at Honor Oak was the site of an early environmental protest over a hundred years ago. The campaign to keep the wooded hillside free for the enjoyment of the general public lasted from 1896 to 1905.

This land was part of the ancient Great North Wood. Until the autumn of 1896, when it was quietly and effectively enclosed by a golf club, the hill had always been a popular open space which people enjoyed visiting. The erection of a 6 ft fence caused a storm of indignation. A number of meetings protesting against the enclosure were held in 1897 on Peckham Rye. Consequently the 'Enclosure of Honor Hill Protest Committee' was formed. The committee, which had 23 members at its first meeting, rapidly grew to around 150.

One Sunday in 1897 around 15,000 people assembled at various points in the vicinity of the hill. Some people pulled down part of the fence and soon the hill was covered with a disorderly multitude. It was quickly found necessary to reinforce the police who had been posted to keep order.

An even bigger crowd of between 50,000 and 100,000 gathered on 17 October 1897. Around 500 police, on foot and mounted, tried to keep order. Stones were thrown and a police inspector was badly wounded. After further agitation and intense campaigning, Camberwell Borough Council arranged with the London County Council for a clause to be inserted in their General Powers Bill 1902 for the compulsory acquisition of One Tree Hill. Consequently, since 1905 the hill has been freely used by members of the public.

The Story of the One Tree Hill Agitation by John Nisbet gives details of the campaign.

The official opening day of One Tree Hill, 7 August 1905.

Cox's Walk, Dulwich, c. 1905.

Cox's Walk

This wooded path between Dulwich Common and Sydenham Hill, was created by John Cox who obtained permission in around 1704 to cut a walk through the woods opposite his inn. The Grove Tavern stands on the site of his inn, the Green Man.

In those days fashionable men and women flocked to spas to take the water for the good of their health. Cox's Walk was a short cut from the wells, or spa, in what is now Sydenham Wells Park. In 1739 John Cox's son dug a 60 ft deep well in the grounds of his inn and discovered his own mineral spring. Crowds came not only to drink the waters from 'Dulwich Spa' but also to enjoy many entertainments at the Green Man where Mr Cox had 'a room for breakfasts and dancing' and a bowling green.

Cox's Walk leads to Sydenham Hill Wood where until 1954 trains ran from Lordship Lane station through a tunnel to Crystal Palace High Level station. A footbridge crosses where the tracks used to be. The elegant brick and wood cantilever bridge was renewed with teak in 1908 to the same design of the 1865 original bridge. The French painter Camille Pissarro sat there to paint a picture of Lordship Lane station in 1871.

Foxes forage along Cox's Walk at dusk and some locally uncommon birds are often recorded on the adjacent playing fields – wheatear, ring ouzel and golden plover.

Lucas Gardens

Lucas Gardens were created in the grounds of a former lunatic asylum, Camberwell House. The building dates from 1777 and was formerly known as the East Terrace. This range of houses is of some architectural interest. Henry Roberts was born in one of the houses at the beginning of the nineteenth century. He was the architect of the Fishmongers' Hall and an early employer of George Gilbert Scott who designed the present St Giles's church in Camberwell. A later resident of the houses was Robert Alexander Gray, chairman of the Camberwell Vestry which ran the civic affairs before the Camberwell Borough Council was formed in 1900. He was known as 'Father of the Parish'.

The houses were taken over as an extension of Camberwell House Lunatic Asylum which was on the north side of Peckham Road. This building still exists and is used as an extension to Southwark Town Hall; it dates from around 1780. The building was originally King Alfred School, or Alfred House Academy, founded by Dr Nicolas Wanostrocht. It was the most famous school for the boys in the parish in the late eighteenth and early nineteenth centuries. Some of those educated there included: Robert Browning, father of the poet; mathematician George Parker Bidder; Alfred Dommett, first Prime Minister of New Zealand, and Sir Joseph Arnold, Chief Justice of India. In 1832 the school moved to Blackheath and the Royal Naval School took over the premises. In 1846 the building became a lunatic asylum.

Lucas Gardens in Vestry Road, opened on 28 July 1955 by the chairman of the London County Council, Norman Prichard.

Picture from *The Illustrated London News* of Little Dorrit's Playground, 1902.

Little Dorrit's Playground

Close to Borough Underground station and St George the Martyr church is Little Dorrit's Playground, which opened on 25 January 1902. The name was chosen because of the playground's close proximity to the site of the Marshalsea Prison. The prison and its inmates provided Charles Dickens with the theme for his book *Little Dorrit*. In the novel, published in monthly parts between 1855 and 1857, William Dorrit had been in Marshalsea Prison, due to debt, for so long that he had become 'Father of the Marshalsea'. His situation was alleviated by the devotion of Amy, his youngest daughter nicknamed 'Little Dorrit' who was born in the prison.

Little Dorrit's Playground was created on land previously occupied by Falcon Court. This was described as 'a horrible rookery of tumble-down dirty hovels' which harboured disease and vice. The new tarmacked open space was originally little more than an acre in size. Lord Monkswell, chairman of the Parks and Open Spaces Committee of the London County Council, attended the opening. He said that he hoped those children present who had read *Little Dorrit* would realise that they were more fortunate than the children who used to live near the old Marshalsea Prison. In declaring the playground open, Mr A. Pomeroy-Cragg, London County Councillor for Rotherhithe, remarked that this was the ninety-second open space which the London County Council had cleared and given to London, with a total acreage of 7,909. He suggested that the local county councillors should provide a sandpit for the children. The North London Prize Band performed in the playground before and after the ceremony.

Nunhead Cemetery

The Friends of Nunhead Cemetery perform vital work in preserving an important Victorian cemetery. The annual open day attracts hundreds of people who have a fascinating time visiting stalls and learning about graves, trees and wildlife. Visitors can imagine they are in the heart of the countryside – as they would have been in 1840 when the cemetery opened close to the Surrey hamlet of Nunhead.

Nunhead was one of seven great Victorian cemeteries established in a ring around the outskirts of London. Nunhead Hill, the site chosen for the cemetery, rises to 200 ft above sea level at its highest point. It affords extensive views over the City of London and St Paul's Cathedral in one direction, and towards the North Downs in the other.

The cemetery, known as All Saints', was opened by the London Cemetery Company who owned Highgate Cemetery. The Company suffered from a major scandal in 1865 following the death of its secretary, Edward Buxton, whose grave can still be seen at Nunhead. It was discovered that he had been engaged in various frauds for many years, and had embezzled over £18,000 of the company's money – a vast amount in those days.

The company recovered from this setback but fortunes declined after the First World War. This was partly because people spent less on burials and the lavish funerals of earlier years became less popular. There were also growing maintenance costs. In 1969 the United Cemeteries Ltd closed the cemetery which was left to decay and slowly return to nature. In due course Southwark Council bought the cemetery for £1 and the Friends of Nunhead Cemetery was formed to resurrect the cemetery. The organization has produced interesting and informative publications including *More Nunhead Notables* by Ron Woollacott and *The Leysdown Tragedy*, *Nunhead Remembered* and *Nunhead and the Music Hall* by Rex Batten.

All Saints' Cemetery, *c.* 1845.

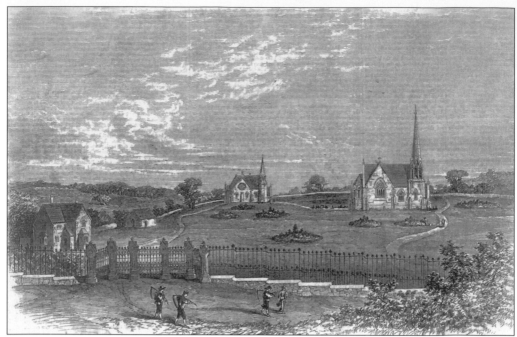

Camberwell Old Cemetery, 1856.

Camberwell Old Cemetery

This cemetery in Forest Hill Road was opened in 1856 by Camberwell Vestry which ran local affairs in the nineteenth century. Unusually for a cemetery of this size (around thirty-eight acres) three chapels were built – Church of England, Nonconformist and Roman Catholic. Unfortunately not one of them still exists as they were all damaged during bombing in the Second World War.

The Anglican and Nonconformist chapels were designed by one of the foremost architects of the day, George Gilbert Scott, who had designed Camberwell's parish church of St Giles. Only a large Gothic lodge now remains of the original cemetery buildings. There is an impressive First World War memorial close to the entrance.

Among the many people buried in the cemetery are: James Berkeley who was trained by engineer Robert Stephenson and built the first railway line in India; Rebekah Horniman who was the first wife of F.J. Horniman, a tea merchant and founder of the Horniman Museum; Richard Wallis, who for sixty-three years was clerk to Camden Chapel in Peckham Road (where Voltaire is today); Charles Waters who founded the International Bible Reading Association in 1882 and was manager of the London and County Bank, Kings Cross, for twenty-five years; George Yanni who was convicted of murdering three Armenians who are also buried in the same cemetery. The men were killed in 1903 as part of the political intrigue involving the Armenian club in Peckham Rye, which was a front for a secret society dedicated to freeing Armenia from Turkish rule.

Camberwell Old Cemetery was written by Ron Woollacott.

Six
People

Dr Salter

Dr Salter was a popular doctor who served as Member of Parliament for Bermondsey for over twenty years. The inspiring story of his life is told in *Bermondsey Story: the Life of Alfred Salter* by Fenner Brockway.

Dr Alfred Salter and Charles Ammon MP drinking fruit juice at an open-air gathering in Southwark Park in 1937 to promote the benefits of an alcohol-free lifestyle.

Donald Soper and Sister Margaret Dix at a Harvest Festival in the late 1920s.

Lord Soper

Lord Soper spoke at Tower Hill and in Hyde Park almost every week until he was ninety-five. He started speaking there when he was minister of Oakley Place Wesleyan church from 1926 until 1929.

Immediately after leaving Cambridge University he became a probationer Methodist minister in the church just off the Old Kent Road. One of his first experiences involved a man who announced to his family that he was going to cut his throat. The Revd Donald Soper was just about to preside over the women's meeting when the deaconess heard about the man with the razor and rushed to fetch the young minister.

'When I got there,' recalled Donald Soper many years later, 'he was standing in the middle of the room, drunk and brandishing his razor. There were one or two children in various corners of the room. I offered to shake hands with him and luckily he put the razor down to shake hands with me, and then one of the kids nipped off with the razor and was two streets away before he could say *knife*.'

Places like Rivet Street, where the man lived, were to Donald Soper a revelation of horrors unimagined. When Soper was at Cambridge University he was academically aware of what words like poverty, deprivation and poor housing meant but actually to see those things came as a profound shock to him. He had not been trained to cope with what he found in the Old Kent Road area.

The story of how Donald Soper started speaking at Tower Hill whilst a minister at Oakley Place Wesleyan church is told in *The Bitter Cry Heard and Heeded: The Story of the South London Mission*.

Michael Faraday

On the main island at the Elephant & Castle is an inscription which reads: 'This stainless steel sculpture commemorates Michael Faraday (1791-1867) English chemist and physicist known for his research into electricity and magnetism who lived locally.' Faraday was born on 22 September 1791 in Newington Butts and was the son of a blacksmith.

The *South London Press* reported on 8 May 1959: 'The Michael Faraday memorial, in the form of a disguised London Transport electricity sub-station at the Elephant and Castle, is to be planned and built by the LCC even though the money needed has not yet been raised by the organizing committee.'

The Michael Faraday Memorial Library was established by the Metropolitan Borough of Southwark and opened on 28 October 1927 by Sir Oliver Lodge. A brochure in Southwark Local Studies Library, produced to mark the library's opening, states: 'Faraday's fundamental discoveries in the realm of magnetism and electricity have given rise to the various applications of the electrical sciences as we know them today.' The library contained 1,800 books devoted to the life and work of Faraday, together with textbooks dealing with magnetism, electrical engineering, and the many allied sciences.

A bust of Michael Faraday was unveiled on 17 October 1928 by Lt-Col. Kenelm Edgecumbe at the Central Public Library, Walworth Road (now Newington Library). The bust was the gift of the Institution of Electrical Engineers.

The Cuming Museum has the Faraday family Bible in which Michael's father wrote the dates of birth of Michael and his brothers and sisters, also an early electric dynamo used by Faraday. Michael Faraday School joined in the nationwide celebrations which marked the Faraday Bicentenary in 1991. The scientist's grave is in Highgate Cemetery. Michael Faraday is included in *Re-weaving Rainbows: Some Southwark Science Tales and Pilgrimage Walk* by D.H. Leaback.

The Michael Faraday memorial electricity sub-station is seen here around 1972.

View in Southwark Park, c. 1900, showing the memorial fountain erected in memory of Jabez West.

Jabez West

A memorial fountain was erected in Southwark Park in 1885 to commemorate Jabez West, a well-known teetotaller who was concerned about the drink problem in the nineteenth century. Jabez West was born at Princes Risborough in 1810 and became an apprentice to a fellmonger, a dealer in skins of animals. He went to London in 1836 and settled in Bermondsey where he followed his trade in the skin yards. In 1838 he joined the Temperance party and was at once recognized as a good platform man and soon became famous as a speaker. He worked incessantly, addressing meetings all over the Home Counties.

In religion he was a nonconformist and in politics was a staunch Liberal. He was prominent in the early days of the Chartist movement and was one of the first members of the first Southwark Liberal Association. He assisted in returning to Parliament Alderman Humphery, Mr Apsley Pellatt (after whom Pellatt Road SE22 was named) and Sir William Molesworth.

George Oliver wrote *The Story of the West Memorial Fountain* in which he stated: 'One evening, perhaps a year or more before the death of the old veteran, he, my dear old friend, Enoch Benson, and myself, were returning from a meeting of the Southwark Temperance Union in the Borough, and when passing Old Bermondsey church he pointed to the drinking fountain built in the wall of the churchyard lodge, remarking that he thought "those things had done more for the temperance cause than all the talking done by the advocates". Benson said, "When you die, Jabez, we will erect one to your memory".' Jabez West died in 1884.

Seven

Places of Worship

Bermondsey Abbey

Bermondsey had an abbey which was one of the greatest religious houses in the country though originally there was a small monastery, of which nothing is left, which was established in around 700 AD by monks from the Abbey of St Peter at Peterborough. A new monastery, founded in 1082, became the Bermondsey Abbey and although there are no remains above ground, much is known about it from old pictures, documents and archaeological discoveries.

The Abbey's founder was Aylwin Child, a citizen of London, who in 1082 gave the rents of some property in the City to the monastery of La Charité on the River Loire in France. In 1089 monks from La Charité started a monastery in Bermondsey at the invitation of the Archbishop of Canterbury, Lanfranc. Its new and beautiful church was dedicated to the Holy Saviour so it was known as St Saviour's.

Cluny Place, close to Bermondsey Central Hall, is a reminder that La Charité came under an even more famous religious house, the Abbey of Cluny in eastern France. The Bermondsey monks belonged to the Cluniac order.

At first Bermondsey was known as a priory because it was under a prior who was subject to the Abbot of Cluny. In 1399 it became Bermondsey Abbey when an Englishman, John Attilburgh, became Abbot. The Abbey came to an end in 1538 when Henry VIII dissolved the monasteries in England.

Sir Thomas Pope bought the abbey church and demolished it. With the stones he built himself a mansion known as Bermondsey House. Some stone from the Abbey is in the Cuming Museum.

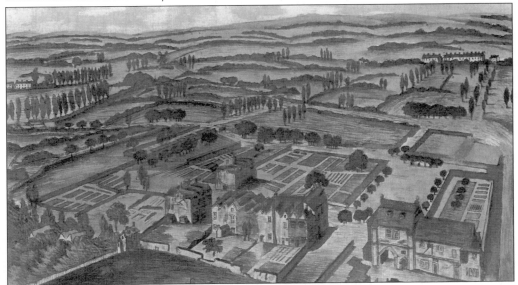

Drawing of Bermondsey Abbey, c. 1805.

Southwark Cathedral, c. 1910.

Southwark Cathedral

This cathedral is the oldest building in the London Borough of Southwark. There has been a church on the site for nearly 1,000 years, although there is no reliable evidence about the origin of the present cathedral. The first documentary evidence is in the *Domesday Book* of 1086. It was rebuilt in 1106 and then again a century later after a fire. The tower seen in the above picture was completed in 1520. The bells have been recast from those which were rung in 1577 when Queen Elizabeth I attended a wedding nearby.

In the Middle Ages the church was part of the Priory of St Mary Overie (meaning 'over the river' or 'on the river') and was run by Augustinian canons. After the dissolution of the monasteries by Henry VIII, the priory church became the parish church of St Saviour. The cloisters were granted to the father of Lord Montague, the site of which is remembered today as Montague Close. In the 1830s the nave fell into disrepair and the church became known as St Saviour's Folly. The nave was rebuilt by Henry Rose in the 1870s and again by Sir Arthur Blomfield between 1890 and 1897. In 1905 St Saviour's became the cathedral for the new diocese of Southwark, which stretches from Richmond in the far west of London, to Woolwich in the east, and as far south as Reigate in Surrey.

St George's Cathedral

The grandfather of former USA President Ronald Reagan was christened in St George's Cathedral. John Reagan was born in Peckham in 1854 but since at that time there wasn't a Roman Catholic church in Peckham he had to be taken to St George's to be baptised. St George's was opened by Bishop Wiseman on 4 July 1848. To mark the occasion, Pope Pius IX sent a golden chalice and paten as a gift.

Two years later St George's was chosen as the cathedral church of the new Diocese of Southwark which was to cover the south-east and the Channel Islands.

St George's was designed by A.W.N. Pugin, the noted architect of the Gothic revival. Unfortunately lack of funds prevented the committee from accepting the first design of a cruciform cathedral on a grand scale, and less ambitious plans had to be prepared.

Disaster came during the massive air raids during the Second World War. On 16 April 1941 an incendiary bomb set light to the roof and in minutes the cathedral was ablaze from end to end; the next day it was a smouldering ruin. Only when restoration work began in 1953 did the full extent of the fire damage became apparent. Few parts of the original building were sound enough to be incorporated in the reconstructed cathedral. On 4 July 1958 the new building was opened by Bishop Cowderoy. Pope John Paul II visited the Cathedral in 1982.

A colourful guide, *St George's Cathedral Southwark*, is available from the cathedral.

St George's Cathedral, *c.* 1910.

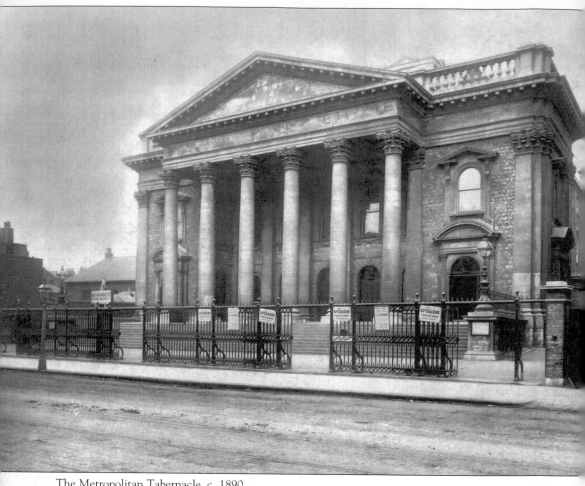

The Metropolitan Tabernacle, *c.* 1890.

Spurgeon's Tabernacle

Thousands of travellers pass the stone columns of the Metropolitan Tabernacle at the Elephant and Castle every day, unaware of the history of what was once an impressive Victorian church. The original building, opened in 1861, could seat around 5,500 people. The church was built for the famous Baptist preacher Charles Haddon Spurgeon. In 1854 he became pastor of New Park Street Chapel. His arrival soon led to such crowds thronging to the chapel that services had to be moved to a vast hired hall in the Strand, and then to the Royal Surrey Gardens Music Hall, where up to 10,000 people assembled. Charles Haddon Spurgeon was one of the most consistently successful preachers of the Victorian era. Other institutions were formed as a result of Spurgeon's work including a college for pastors, almshouses and an orphanage. The original Tabernacle of Spurgeon's time was burned down in 1898 except for the front portico and basement. It was rebuilt along similar lines but was later burnt down for the second time when hit by an incendiary bomb in the longest air raid of the Second World War in May 1941. Once again the portico and basement survived and the Tabernacle was rebuilt on the original perimeter walls but to a different design. The church was re-opened on 24 October 1959.

Bermondsey Central Hall

Old houses were demolished to make way for Bermondsey Central Hall which was opened in 1900, and built for the South London Mission which celebrated its centenary in 1989. The design of the entrance was based on Tower Bridge which had opened 6 years earlier.

   Though the Central Hall had over 2,000 seats it was not uncommon for hundreds of people to be turned away because it was full and policemen had to control the crowds trying to get in. By the 1960s the large hall was too big for the congregations so it was demolished. Flats were built on the site and a new chapel was made in the former entrance hall. When that became too small for the growing congregation, a larger chapel was created in 2000 in a hall which had been opened in 1931 by Miss Megan Lloyd George for the South London Mission's child welfare and maternity work.

The architect's drawing of Bermondsey Central Hall.

St Giles's parish church.

St Giles's Church

St Giles's, the impressive parish church of Camberwell, was consecrated in 1844. It was designed by Sir George Gilbert Scott who was the architect of St Pancras Hotel and the Albert Memorial.

St Giles's is famous for its beautiful east window which is a rare survival of stained glass whose design was strongly influenced by John Ruskin, after whom Ruskin Park was named. From the nave the window looks like a mosaic of bright colours. Looked at more closely, from the chancel, it reveals pictures of many Bible stories. In the centre are scenes from the life of Jesus and on the left are Old Testament scenes. The rainbow from the story of Noah's Ark, and Jacob's Ladder, are easy to find.

Ruskin visited the great French cathedrals, Chartres and Rouen, to get ideas for the window and copied their rich colours. The stained glass in the west window of St Giles's is around 700 years old and came from Trier in Germany. It was donated by the Revd George Storie who was vicar when the church was being built.

Another special feature of St Giles's is its organ made by J.C. Bishop, founder of a firm of organ builders. It was designed by Samuel Sebastian Wesley, grandson of hymnwriter Charles Wesley, who had been organist at the old St Giles's church which was destroyed by fire in 1841. It had been built on the site of an Anglo-Saxon church which stood among cornfields, meadows and woodland; its existence was recorded in *Domesday Book*.

St Giles is said to have been a seventh-century hermit who lived in a cave in the south of France. Historian Mary Boast wrote *St Giles: the Parish Church of Camberwell*.

Christ Church

Behind Christ Church, the headquarters of the South London Industrial Mission, Blackfriars Road, is a stone cross marking the place where the burning cross from the old church fell during Second World War.

The original church on the site was erected under an Act of Parliament passed in the reign of King Charles II. The site of the parish was formerly called the Liberty, or Manor, of Paris Garden, in the parish of St Saviour, Southwark. The church was founded under the terms of the will of John Marshall who bequeathed £700 for the building of a new church and the purchase of a churchyard. The land that was purchased belonged to William Angel who conveyed it to the trustees in 1670. The original church was erected and consecrated in 1671.

In 1737 the representatives of Mr Marshall's trustees applied to Parliament to rebuild the church and steeple. The new church was built between 1738 and 1741. Unfortunately this church was destroyed on 17 April 1941 but a new church and Industrial Mission Centre was opened on 24 February 1960 by the Duke of Edinburgh. Inside the modern premises are beautiful stained glass windows with pictures of Southwark workers including a boatman on the Thames, a printer with his press, an engineer with machinery and a secretary in her office with a cleaner. The main meeting room is called John Marshall Hall.

A coloured brochure called *Windows on the World of Work* showing the attractive windows is available from the South London Industrial Mission.

Christ Church, *c.* 1850.

St George's church, c. 1910.

St George's Church

The former St George's church in Wells Way was converted in 1993 into thirty one-bedroom flats, built around a central courtyard. The building had been disused since 1970 and had been gutted by fire and vandalism.

A windmill stood close to the church at a time when it was built among green fields. In 1820 there were 1,394 inhabited houses in the district of Camberwell with an average of five people in each. As there was accommodation for only 1,300 worshippers in St Giles' parish church, it was decided to build a new church which would hold 2,000 people.

The first stone was laid on the feast of St George, 23 April 1822, by the Lord Bishop of Winchester, Dr George Pretyman-Tomline. He also consecrated the church on St George's Day in 1824.

St George's was one of several large churches erected soon after the Battle of Waterloo which saw the end of long wars against Napoleon. The architect was Francis Bedford who lived in Camberwell Grove. It was built in classical style, similar to the temples of ancient Greece. The interior had three galleries on Greek Doric columns. The total cost was over £20,600, of which £5,000 was contributed by the commissioners for building churches and chapels. The ground was donated by John Rolls.

An apse by Basil Champneys was added in 1893, when the choir was raised and internal embellishments were made in 1909. The present St George's church, in Coleman Road, was dedicated by the Bishop of Southwark in 1982.

St James's Church

Travellers passing through Bermondsey know St James's church, Thurland Road, as an important landmark yet it was threatened with demolition.

After the Battle of Waterloo, Parliament gave permission for £1½ million to be spent on the construction of churches as a thanksgiving for peace and as a memorial to the soldiers who had been killed. Through the persistence of a group of Bermondsey churchmen, the needs of that area were pressed. In 1821 land was bought and a generous grant was obtained from the commissioners who controlled the fund for the building of new churches granted after 1815. Building was delayed for six years because the committee wanted a tower and a spire but there was not enough money to build them. They devised a scheme which involved building a crypt under the church in which bodies could be buried; this provided a steady income.

The architect of what has been described as 'the grandest church in Bermondsey' was James Savage. The church was modelled on Greek Temples with galleries around three sides and the organ, built by J.C. Bishop, in the west. The spire was copied from Sir Christopher Wren's at St Stephen Walbrook in the City of London. The church was consecrated by Dr Charles Richard Sumner, Bishop of Winchester, on 7 May 1829 and could hold 2,000 people.

By the 1960s the crumbling fabric of the church was causing concern and there appeared to be no alternative to demolition but thankfully a way was found to restore this impressive building. Sir John Betjeman said: 'Of all the churches built in London by the Waterloo Commission, it is the finest, the most original and the most impressive.'

St James's church.

St Peter's church, c. 1931.

St Peter's Church

Walworth's oldest church building is St Peter's church in Liverpool Grove. It was designed by one of the greatest of all English architects, Sir John Soane. Other buildings by him include parts of the Bank of England and Dulwich Picture Gallery.

St Peter's was the first of Sir John Soane's three London churches, each of which resembles the other two. St Peter's, opened in 1825, bears a particular likeness to Holy Trinity, Marylebone. St John on Bethnal Green was his other church.

When St Peter's was built, Walworth had developed as an elegant Georgian suburb. There was insufficient space for worshippers in the old parish church of St Mary Newington and so St Peter's was built. Like other churches set up as a result of the Waterloo Commission, St Peter's is in the style of an ancient Greek temple, with columns before the entrance but it also has an unusual tower which stands out above the rooftops of the small streets around it and makes a landmark for people looking down from the tall blocks of the Aylesbury Estate. The white marble font, where babies have been christened since 1839, was made by Garland and Fieldwick, a local firm of masons.

When a bomb fell directly on the church in the Second World War, eighty-four people were killed while sheltering in the crypt. In 1953 the restoration was completed by T.F. Ford.

Holy Trinity

Trinity Church Square has changed little during the last 150 years and is one of the most attractive conservation areas in the London Borough of Southwark. Holy Trinity was one of the new churches built in the 1820s to provide for the rapidly growing population of South London. It was designed by Francis Bedford, an architect who also designed St George's, Wells Way.

Holy Trinity Church was consecrated in 1824. Despite being damaged in the Second World War, it continued to be used as a church until 1959 and is reputed to be the subject of the music hall song *At Trinity Church I met me doom.*

The statue in front of the church has been subject to speculation but it has now been confirmed that it was originally at Westminster Hall. It was possibly made in the fourteenth century and much repaired in later centuries. It is said to represent King Alfred but there is no evidence to support that theory.

Trinity Church Square, which was built between 1825 and about 1832 in uniform style, is a fine example of early nineteenth century architecture. The land belongs to the Corporation of Trinity House to whom it was conveyed in 1661 by Christopher Merrick, a London Merchant, 'for relieving – the poor, aged, sick, maimed, weak and decayed seamen and marines of this kingdom, their wives, children and widows.'

In recent years the building has been very well restored to serve as a rehearsal hall for two London orchestras and is now known as the Henry Wood Hall.

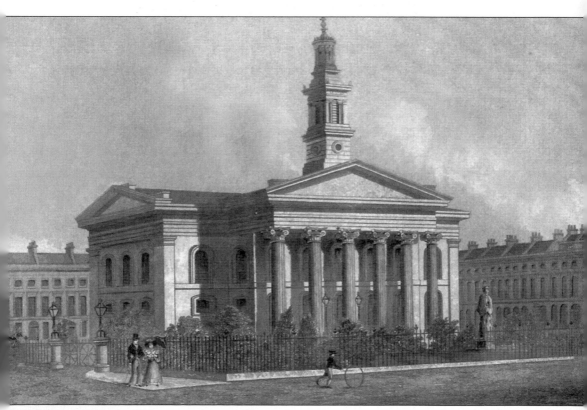

Holy Trinity Church, 1830.

St George the Martyr church, c. 1925.

St George the Martyr Church

The church of St George the Martyr, close to Borough Underground station, was rebuilt in 1736 by the architect John Price. There had been a church on the site since at least 1122, when the right to appoint the rector was given to Bermondsey Abbey.

The ceiling of the present church was designed by Basil Champneys in 1897 and renewed after wartime damage. It shows the Glory of God breaking through the clouds. The bells and the organ are from the older church and some of the old stones are on show in the crypt. The font is a replica of the old one. Registers dating from 1602 to the present day record christenings, marriages and burials. On the wall are memorials to people who lived in the parish. The open space across Tabard Street was once part of the burial ground.

St George the Martyr church is also known as *Little Dorrit's church*. According to the novel by Charles Dickens, Little Dorrit lived with her father in Marshalsea Prison where Dickens's own father had once been imprisoned. One night, returning home late, Little Dorrit slept in the church vestry using one of the old registers as a pillow. The modern east window has a small picture of Little Dorrit.

In 1868 it was decided to have the church clock lit by gas lighting but, to save money, only three of the four faces were lit. One face is still black, although the church is now lit by electricity.

St George the Martyr church, a major London landmark for centuries, is now in danger of collapsing because of structural problems. Over £3 million is needed to save the church and to create exciting new facilities for the community.

Eight
Public Services

Newington Vestry Hall

The former Vestry Hall of the local government parish of St Mary Newington stands in Walworth Road at the corner of Wansey Street. The site had belonged to the Fishmongers' Company of the City of London. The building was designed by Henry Jarvis, a prolific local architect who lived in Trinity Square. The official opening took place on 8 August 1865.

A report of the opening ceremony was published in the *South London Press* which stated that there were arguments at the previous week's Vestry meeting about the programme. The newspaper reported that 'the pruning knife cut deeply into the arrangements'. The 7th Surrey Rifle Band was cut out of the programme and the Church of England clergymen were allowed to take part on condition that dissenters were included.

The Vestrymen marched from their old meeting place in St Mary Newington School for the official opening but there was not the slightest sign of interest shown by the ratepayers in the procession. Various speeches were made inside the new Vestry Hall. The Revd Mr Turquand claimed that everyone would agree that the building combined three qualities – utility, solidity and beauty.

The proceedings, which were listened to with much interest by people in the crowded gallery, were brought to a close by several rounds of enthusiastic cheers for the architect, builders, chairman, clerks and the other officials. From the hall the Vestrymen and other people were taken by horse-drawn omnibuses to the Greyhound Inn at Dulwich for a dinner.

The Vestry Hall, 1866.

The power station, Bankside, 1961.

Bankside Power Station

The power station was designed by Sir Giles Gilbert Scott and completed in 1963. It was the last power station to be built in central London and also the last of the huge brick power stations which began with Battersea. It burnt oil instead of the dirtier coal.

The idea of building a colossal power station right across the Thames from St Paul's Cathedral was deeply shocking, especially in the immediate post-war context of trying to plan a new clean and bright London full of open spaces and wide roads, with heavy industry zoned to less conspicuous areas. The London County Council's County of London Plan (1945) envisaged Bankside with a park along the river and commercial buildings behind.

However, Bankside had been an industrial area for centuries, with wharves and warehouses lining the Thames, and the new power station was built merely to replace the old one. The City of London Electric Lighting Co Ltd had first built a power station on the site in 1891 and this had been much enlarged in 1928. The central chimney of Scott's Bankside Power Station is 325 ft tall compared with 370 ft to the top of the cross on St Paul's Cathedral.

The Bankside Power Station closed in 1981 and was converted into the Tate Modern art gallery, which opened in 2000.

Old Age Pensions

Pensioners throughout Britain have reason to be grateful for a movement that began in Walworth at the Robert Browning Settlement. The organization's first warden, the Revd Francis Herbert Stead, was concerned that old people were being treated unfairly. He wrote: 'Many old people come to me begging for work... anything to keep me from the workhouse. What kind of people are these? Not thriftless, but respectable, sober, honest, hard-working men and women who have brought up families, but in old age find themselves destitute. The moment someone ceases to be of value as an economic tool, they are flung aside as worthless.'

Stead called a meeting at Browning Hall (burnt down in 1978), in York Street (renamed Browning Street). Four hundred people crowded in to hear a speaker from New Zealand talk about a government pension scheme already started in that country. Stead realised that only an Act of Parliament could bring about real improvement in Britain so he began a nationwide campaign that went on for ten years.

In 1899 a national committee was formed with its headquarters at Browning Hall. In 1908 victory was won. The Government passed the first Old Age Pensions Act. This allowed all people over seventy to be given a state pension of 5s a week.

The Robert Browning Settlement, which continues to do important work today, was started in 1895. Its roots lie in the York Street Chapel which became Browning Hall, named after the poet Robert Browning who was baptised in the chapel. After his death, members of the chapel and other benefactors decided to start a social and religious settlement as a world memorial to one of England's greatest poets.

Browning Hall in 1978.

The post office, Peckham High Street, c. 1905.

The Post Office

The post office in Peckham High Street was built to replace one which was damaged in the Second World War, but later repaired. Behind it stood the SE District Sorting Office. Information about the early postal arrangements for Peckham are scanty. This Surrey village was in the London Penny Post area, just within the three mile limit, and under the control of the Southwark office. A map of 1697 by Ralph Blackhall, a collector of the Penny Post, would seem to indicate that letters from Peckham were routed through the neighbouring village of Camberwell.

From as early as 1684 there were two Receiving Houses in Peckham. One was no doubt in the High Street and the other at Peckham Rye. The latter was in an area where wealthy people lived and they would be the ones most likely to write letters.

In 1792 George Hurst was appointed letter-man for the Peckham district and continued to act in this capacity until around 1842. He died in 1852 at the age of ninety-four.

With the reorganisation of the London Post Office in 1794, the Penny Post was brought into line with the General Post. Letters could then be sent either paid or unpaid. At that time Peckham had three deliveries and collections at 9.15 a.m. and 4.15 p.m.

The Peckham Sorting Office which took over the postmarking of letters was opened in the 1890s in Hanover Street (now Highshore Road) on land now occupied by the present Royal Mail Sorting Office which also incorporates the front of the former Quaker Meeting House which was opened in 1826.

Wash-houses

A plaque on the former baths and wash-houses in Wells Way, SE5, commemorates the stone laying by Lady Llangattock on 25 July 1901. She also performed the formal opening ceremony in May 1903 because her husband gave the land to Camberwell Borough Council.

John Passmore Edwards contributed £3,000 towards the cost of the library on the same site. This had a newspaper reading room and a reference reading room as well as a lending section.

The baths accommodated fifty slipper baths. In *The Story of Camberwell*, Mary Boast stated that North Camberwell public baths and wash-houses were much appreciated by people living nearby in houses with no bathrooms, washing machines or constant hot water. In *Times of our Lives* Stan Hall recalled, 'We had baths in Wells Way, quite close to our home. For 3d you were supplied with a square of soap and what appeared to be a length of corrugated paper (they said it was a towel)... Inside ... you were in a large space with cubicles of black stone, open-topped... The attendant would lead you to one of them. Inside was a large bath of the same colour. The attendant would use a key to turn a tap outside and a flow of water would enter the baths... shouts could be heard for "A drop more hot for No. 6," or "More cold in No. 13," etc. as well as curses should cold be turned on when hot was wanted.'

The North Camberwell Public Library closed in 1991. It is now used by Groundwork Southwark which has published a book by Tim Charlesworth on Burgess Park. This early twentieth century building now stands in the park.

North Camberwell public baths and wash-houses, 1977.

Inner London Crown Court, 1978.

Gaol and Court

Inner London Crown Court in Newington Causeway was opened on 11 January 1921 as the Sessions House for the County of London. Inside in the Justices' Room is a chimney piece taken from Hicks Hall, Finsbury, dating from 1612. The present court was damaged by enemy action during the Second World War and repaired in 1954.

Behind the court is Newington Gardens which is known locally as Gaol Park. This is because it stands where the Surrey County Gaol (also known as Horsemonger Lane Gaol) used to be. In 1791 the Surrey Justices purchased $3\frac{1}{2}$ acres of market garden ground in Newington on which to build a new County Gaol and Sessions House. The ground abutted on Horsemonger Lane (now known as Harper Road). The prison consisted of a quadrangle of three storeys, three sides being used for criminals and the fourth for debtors. Provision was made for over 400 prisoners.

Leigh Hunt, the English poet and essayist, spent part of his two-year sentence for libel in Horsemonger Lane Gaol between 1813 and 1815 and was visited there by Lord Byron and Charles Lamb.

Charles Dickens witnessed the public execution of the Mannings there in 1849 and expressed his disgust in a letter to *The Times*, thus beginning the agitation against public executions which culminated in their abolition in 1868.

The prison was closed in 1878. Two years later the inner area was cleared and, in 1884, just over an acre of land was opened by Mrs Gladstone as a children's playground. The remainder of the prison buildings were demolished in 1892.

Fire Brigade

Winchester House, where the London Fire Brigade Museum is based in Southwark Bridge Road, was built in 1820 for Mr John Rawlinson Harris, who became MP for Southwark. Before that the land, and the land occupied by the Brigade's training centre, was used in 1770 for a popular resort known as 'Finch's Grotto'. This had gardens, orchestral music, firework displays and a health spa. Eventually the owner went bankrupt and in place of the gardens a parish workhouse was built.

At the beginning of the nineteenth century Mr Rawlinson Harris bought the property and workhouse which he converted into a hat factory and built Winchester House as his home. It was so named because it stood on ground which had been part of the Bishop of Winchester's estate in the Middle Ages.

Winchester House and surrounding land were acquired in 1866 by the Metropolitan Board of Works so a headquarters could be built for its newly formed Metropolitan Fire Brigade. One of the world's most illustrious fire fighters, Capt. (later Sir) Eyre Massey Shaw, took up residence in Winchester House and lived there until his retirement in 1891. It then became the home of his successor and subsequent chief officers for a further forty-six years.

On opening the new headquarters at Lambeth in 1937, the chief officer moved his quarters but during the Second World War Winchester House was occupied by several fire officers.

Winchester House now houses one of the most comprehensive collections of firefighting equipment and memorabilia in the country. It details the progression of the London Fire Brigade from the days of James Braidwood, the first commander of the London Fire Engine Establishment on its formation in 1833.

Winchester House.

Beachcroft Reservoir under construction.

Honor Oak Reservoir

At Honor Oak is the largest brick-built underground reservoir in Europe – Beachcroft Reservoir, officially opened on 5 May 1909 by the Lord Mayor of London, the Right Honourable Sir George Wyatt Truscott. The reservoir was named after Sir Melvill Beachcroft, the first chairman of the Metropolitan Water Board which became operational in 1904.

Four hundred men spent three years constructing the reservoir. The 19 million bricks used in building it were made from clay excavated on the site and it was hailed as the largest and finest in the world when it was completed. The reservoir is split into four cells and has a total capacity of 56 million gallons. The drinking water is pumped from Honor Oak to other service reservoirs around south-east London from where it flows by gravity on a ring main into customers' homes. The reservoir stores treated drinking water from Surbiton, Walton and Hampton Water Treatment Works.

During the 1990s a £3 million improvement programme was carried out; national newspapers showed pictures of the inside of the huge empty reservoir.

On top of the reservoir is the Aquarius Golf Club which was established in 1912. The name Aquarius was taken from the magazine of the Metropolitan Water Board Staff Association. When a boy called Henry Cotton was eight years old he became a junior member of the Aquarius Golf Club. Within three years he was so proficient that the club made him a full member. He won the Club championship before reaching his teens. He won the Open Championship three times and was the first British golfer to be knighted.

Nine

Recreation

Clubland

Long before he founded the Salvation Army, William Booth attended Walworth Wesleyan chapel which was opened in 1813. Over a century later it was demolished so Clubland could be built. The person who had the vision to build exciting club premises in a deprived part of South London was a young minister, the Revd James Butterworth, who worked tirelessly in Walworth for fifty-four years. In 1922 he started a club with six boys, one room and no money.

Soon hundreds joined and after a few years a rundown court was demolished. A new chapel and clubs were built on the site. They were opened by the Lord Mayor of London, Sir Kynaston Studd, on 1 October 1929. In the 1930s, adjoining property was demolished so a gym, theatre, art studio and workshops could be built.

The premises were opened 20 May 1939 but, sadly, a few months later the Second World War began and Clubland was destroyed on 10 May 1941. Jimmy Butterworth wrote that 'bombs destroyed twenty years' work in as many seconds'.

It was harder in the next twenty-five years to rebuild Clubland than it had been to create it the first time. There was no money and an untrained membership. Lecture tours across Britain and America were organized in order to raise money. Eventually Jimmy Butterworth fulfilled his ambition to rebuild Clubland. The new premises were opened by Her Majesty Queen Elizabeth, the Queen Mother, on 18 May 1964.

Hundreds of young people from the Walworth area have reason to be grateful for Clubland and its many activities which have helped to develop their talents as well as providing them with much enjoyment and fun.

Her Majesty Queen Mary opened the completed premises of Clubland on 20 May 1939.

A sketch of the giraffes and their Nubian attendants, Surrey Zoological Gardens, 1843.

Walworth Zoo

Three years after the London Zoo began, a zoo opened in Walworth in 1831. It was called the Royal Surrey Zoological Gardens and the proprietor was Edward Cross who moved his menagerie from its original home in the Strand. The zoo had lions, tigers, elephants, reindeer, llamas, a pair of dromedaries presented by the ruler of Egypt, and a giant tortoise on which children were able to ride. Five giraffes were brought from Africa by an Arab boy called Fadlallah. A model of them is in the Cuming Museum. In 1848 Queen Victoria, Prince Albert and the royal children paid the zoo a visit. They were especially interested in a rather unusual animal friendship – a tigress and a dog who lived in the same cage.

The zoo closed in 1856 and nothing of it remains in the Manor Place area, where it was situated.

Herne Hill Stadium

Herne Hill Stadium in Burbage Road still runs various cycling activities over a hundred years after it came into being in 1892 due to the efforts of a great racing cyclist, George Lacey-Hillier who floated a company called the London County Athletic Ground Limited. The stadium was built by Peacocks of Water Lane, Brixton, who held the lease until 1945.

There was a cinder track on the inside of the cycle track which was used for athletics. In 1896 a concrete track, $3\frac{1}{2}$ laps to the mile, 30ft wide and with good bankings at each end, was laid and it was considered to be one of the fastest tracks in the world. The great events of the early years included 24-hour races in 1892, 1893 and 1894 when the crowds were estimated to be 20,000.

During the Second World War the grounds were taken over by the RAF as a balloon base. During this period the old cement track cracked up. Thanks to the interest and influence of the Hon. Philip Noel Baker permission was granted to patch up the old cement and cover the whole track with bitumen. This made it possible to hold the 1948 Olympic Games cycle events at Herne Hill.

In 1945 the lease was acquired from Peacocks by the National Cyclists Union but its maintenance and running costs became increasingly expensive so the Greater London Council was persuaded to take the stadium over in 1959. Herne Hill Stadium is London's only stadium with a track for cycle racing and it is England's oldest cycling track. It was totally redeveloped in 1992 and is now a magnificent 450 metre banked oval, constructed of all weather concrete. It is reputed to be the fastest outdoor track in the United Kingdom.

This donkey parade was held at Herne Hill Stadium in around 1910.

Bermondsey Settlement, 1894.

Bermondsey Settlement

The Settlement was in Farncombe Street close to where Scott Lidgett Crescent is today. The Revd John Scott Lidgett launched the plans for a Settlement in 1889 in Cambridge where he was a minister. Bermondsey was chosen for the Settlement because it was the most neglected neighbourhood of poorer London as far as the purposes that Scott Lidgett had in mind. When he visited large firms in Bermondsey, while trying to raise funds, his reception was 'chilly in the extreme'. However, Colonel S.B. Bevington, who became the first Mayor of Bermondsey, encouraged him.

Despite many obstacles and disappointments, the foundation stone was laid in 1891 by Sir Joseph Savory. The main Settlement building was opened for educational work the following year by Sir John Lubbock, chairman of the London County Council. That there was an urgent need for the Settlement was shown in a pathetic letter sent on the eve of the opening. It was written by a young working man who complained: 'Down here in Bermondsey there is nothing between heaven and hell, between the Church and the public house.'

The main object of the Settlement was to bring a force of educated workers to give help to all the higher interests of the neighbourhood – religious, educational, social and administrative. One of the residents was Dr Alfred Salter who met his future wife there. Dr Scott Lidgett was warden for fifty-eight years and the Settlement was demolished in 1969 after effective community service.

The Settlement's history is included in *The Bitter Cry Heard and Heeded* and *A Dictionary of Methodism in Britain and Ireland*.

Nunhead Football Club

Haberdashers' Aske's Hatcham College Playing Fields are where Nunhead Football Club used to play at Brown's Ground. Nunhead FC was Dulwich Hamlet Football Club's closest neighbour and fiercest rival. When Dulwich Hamlet's previous ground at Dog Kennel Hill was opened in 1931, the Nunhead team were their first opponents. An incredible crowd of 16,254 paid to see the old rivals battle out a 1-1 draw.

Nunhead FC, originally known as Shaftesbury and then as Wingfield House, was founded as a club for working boys by a number of gentlemen connected with the Stock Exchange. The club was later divided into two sections, Eastern and Western. In 1895-1896 the Eastern used to meet Dulwich Hamlet, Dulwich St Peter's and Clapham in the Camberwell and Brixton League. Western played Clapham Hawthorne, Willow Dene and Wimbledon Old Centrals in the Clapham League.

Before the start of the 1904-1905 season Wingfield House changed its name to Nunhead having amalgamated with Honor Oak FC. Nunhead FC then played at the Ivy Ground. In 1907 Nunhead FC moved to Brown's Ground which was its home until it disbanded in 1942 after its benefactor's timber firm was destroyed in the Blitz.

Ron Woollacott in *A Historical Tour of Nunhead and Peckham Rye* recalls that it was a training ground for many great footballers including Leslie Henley who played for Nunhead and Arsenal; John Henry Flockton who played at inside left as an amateur for Nunhead and Crystal Palace (and as a cricketer he played for Surrey); Dennis Compton, the great cricketer and footballer, who played as a left winger for Nunhead before signing as an amateur for Arsenal in 1932; Reg Lewis, another great Arsenal footballer, who gained his experience as an amateur with Nunhead.

The story of the club is told in *Nunhead Football Club 1888-1949* by Mick Blakeman.

Nunhead Football Club ground, *c*. 1920.

South London Fine Art Gallery, Camberwell, early twentieth century.

South London Gallery

Over a century ago South London Gallery in Peckham Road was built to house a collection of paintings by eminent artists of the day. The paintings were largely donated to the collection by the artists themselves or by wealthy benefactors. One aim of the gallery was to enable working people to have the opportunity to see the best art being produced at the time. The gallery's founder was William Rossiter; in 1868 he set up a South London Working Men's College at No. 91 Blackfriars Road. Ten years later it moved to larger premises at No. 143 Kennington Lane. The College was extended to include a free library, the first in South London. The library opened in October 1878 and a few months later Rossiter added to it by borrowing pictures to cover the walls during the summer months – so the Gallery was born. As time passed the focus of the institution shifted firmly in the direction of the visual arts and this change was recognised. As Rossiter explained, 'so many friends lent pictures, and so many were allowed to remain, that the exhibition intended for a few weeks has now been in existence for about fourteen years, and has become so important that the name of Free Library has been replaced by that of South London Fine Art Gallery.

The Gallery moved to Battersea and then to Camberwell in 1887 to a warehouse at No. 207 Camberwell Road. The South London Fine Art Gallery was built in Peckham Road and opened to the public in May 1891. The story of the Gallery is told in *Art for the People* edited by Giles Waterfield.

The George Inn

The sign of St George as a knight in armour hangs out over the pavement of Borough High Street. The George Inn, with its galleries, looks much like the inns of Shakespeare's day, except that then there would have been galleried buildings surrounding three sides of the inn-yard, instead of only one as there is today. A long time ago Borough High Street was lined with inns like this.

Until 1750, London Bridge was the only bridge across the Thames in London and the street leading to it always had many travellers. At the Borough inns, they could get a drink, a meal, or a bed for the night, before setting out, or at the end of their journeys.

The George Inn is one of the most famous of England's hostelries and is the only galleried coaching inn left in London. The original name of the inn was St George and the Dragon. The date of construction is uncertain but it is marked on a map of 1542 and very clearly on the map of London made by John Rocque in 1746. There was also a reference to it in 1554 when it was the property of a Mr Colet who represented Southwark in Parliament. In his *Survey of London* (1598), John Stow mentioned the George as one of the 'fair inns, for receipt [receipt] of travellers'.

The George Inn, Borough High Street, 1881. This building was built to replace the one burnt in Southwark's great fire of 1676.

Dulwich Picture Gallery.

Dulwich Picture Gallery

This was the first national picture gallery in England. On 12 July 1811 the Governing Body of Dulwich College recorded in its minutes that the late Sir Francis Bourgeois, on his death on 7 January of the same year, had bequeathed to the College 'his valuable collection of pictures', together with £2,000 for the erection of a new Gallery to house them; and that Mrs Desenfans, to whom the collection had been left for life, wished a Gallery to be immediately erected'. The College resolved 'that it is therefore expedient to erect a Gallery without delay, if we have the means to do so.'

Sir John Soane was chosen as architect and the foundations were laid in 1811. Much of the main work on the shell of the building was carried out the following summer. Progress was recorded in a sketchbook kept in the Soane Museum. The Gallery was opened to the public in 1817, however, work continued on the Gallery and the final figure for expenditure, reported in 1822, was £14,222 15s.

Over the years alterations have been made and these are detailed in *Soane and After: The Architecture of Dulwich Picture Gallery* by Giles Waterfield.

Camberwell Baths

Camberwell Baths were opened on 1 October 1892 by the Lord Mayor of London. The *South London Press* reported: 'The Chief Magistrate of the City and his attendant bodyguard descended upon Camberwell amid quite a glow of civic brilliance. The blare of brazen instruments, the prancing and curvetting of sleek City horses, gorgeous equipages, ornately-attired footmen, flags and banners – flying very limp and dank in the moisture-laden air – all tended to lend animation and picturesqueness to the gay scene, while the march of the armed men was sweet music to those who dote upon the military.'

The civic visitors were received at the entrance to the baths in Artichoke Row by a guard of honour of the 1st Surrey Rifles. The building was the second of three which the authorities were determined to erect in the Parliamentary Divisions of North Camberwell, Peckham and Dulwich, with the addition of wash-houses for North Camberwell and Peckham. Dulwich Baths were opened around three months before those at Camberwell. In 1876 Victoria Baths, which had a private proprietor, were opened in Peckham on land where the Peckham Pulse is today.

The first plunge in Camberwell Baths was taken by boys from neighbouring School Board of London Schools – Bellenden Road, Boundary Lane, Colls Road, Cobourg Road, Gloucester Road, Goodrich Road, Hollydale Road, Leipsic Road, Lyndhurst Grove, Nunhead, Peckham Park, Ruby Street and Sumner Road.

Camberwell Baths.

View of Camberwell Hall from the Grove.

Camberwell Hall

Camberwell Hall in Grove Lane was built in 1748 as a tavern but is now a private residence. It was much used in the nineteenth century as a meeting place for religious, social, political and parochial purposes. In its early days it formed part of a public place of entertainment known as the Grove House, a famous country tavern which was well patronised by young people from the City of London. In those days there were extensive gardens surrounding the house.

The assembly room which became known as Camberwell Hall was the scene of many fashionable local balls. Charles Dickens in his *Sketches of Boz* pictured one of them, attended by the Maldertons, two sisters who lived at 'Oak Lodge, Camberwell'. Fêtes of all kinds were held within the spacious grounds of Grove House.

In 1861 C. Steinitz became lessee of Camberwell Hall. In addition to devoting the hall and minor rooms to public meetings, he used part of the building for his business which was the manufacture of parquetry. Some was used in Gad's Hill, the residence of Charles Dickens.

John Ruskin put forward some of his social ideas in his famous lecture on work to the Camberwell Working Men's Institute in the hall on 24 January 1865. The Surrey Floricultural Society held exhibitions in the hall.

In 1984 Camberwell Hall was still being used as a carpet laying warehouse, with a health club in the assembly rooms and there was a plan to build four neo-Georgian houses in its place. It was bought in 1986 by a sculptor who cleared the arcade of industrial clutter and lowered the space in front to restore it to its original look.

Oxford and Bermondsey Club

At the time of Queen Victoria's Diamond Jubilee in 1897 the conviction had been growing in the minds of a small band of men that the University of Oxford owed a debt to its less fortunate neighbours. They were able to take action as a result of the decision of a newly qualified doctor, John Stansfeld, to practise in a very poor part of London. The Oxford and Bermondsey Club was born on a spring day in 1897 as five men huddled under one umbrella on the rain-soaked platform of a grimy railway station in Spa Road (remains of which still exist). Four of the men were either wealthy or well connected – Bishop Knox of Liverpool, a local brewer named Edwin Barclay, a seed merchant called Sutton and Henry Gibbon, an Oxford college chaplain. The fifth man under the umbrella was John Stansfeld, a civil servant who had studied to become a doctor in his spare time. The others showed Stansfeld the streets all around the station and told him there was not a single boys' club in the area. They said that if he would start one they would back him. The doctor jumped at the chance and what followed is outlined in *A Century of the OBC* by Mark Say.

Shakespeare's *Henry V* was performed in the 1920s by Oxford and Bermondsey Club members on the site of the old Globe Theatre. This was one of countless activities arranged by the Club during the last hundred years.

A drawing of Camberwell Fair, c. 1850.

Camberwell Fair

The fair brought 'annual annoyance' until August 1855 when it was stopped. Camberwell Green was then 'encumbered for the last time with its horde of nomadic thieves; its coarse men and lewd women; and this concentrated essence of vice, folly, and buffoonery was no longer allowed to contaminate the youth of the district and annoy the more staid and respectable residents', according to W.H. Blanch's important book *Ye Parish of Camerwell* published in 1875.

Camberwell Fair was held for twenty-three days starting on 9 August and ending on 1 September, the feast of St Giles, the patron saint. In later years it was held from 19-21 August on or near Camberwell Green. For those three days the residents of Camberwell 'were compelled to witness disgusting and demoralising scenes which they were powerless to prevent.'

Although the complaints of the inhabitants against the continuance of the fair were both loud and numerous, it was not until the beginning of the nineteenth century that any determined efforts were made to put an end to it. On 8 May 1823 Camberwell Vestry, which ran local affairs in the nineteenth century, considered whether the fair was authorised by any charter or other lawful authority in order to try to suppress it.

The fair ended as a result of the energetic efforts of a few individuals who raised money among the local gentry to purchase the rights of the lord of the manor. Camberwell Green was then handed over to the parish who undertook to keep it in decent order.

Dulwich Baths

Dulwich Leisure Centre in East Dulwich Road opened in 1892 as Dulwich Baths. About 1,000 people turned out for the official opening. The first person to use the Baths was Mr G.A. Blake, amateur plunging champion of England, who dived into the pool and glided for 63ft 2in, which was 12in below his record. This was followed by a programme of swimming races and a water polo match. Music was provided by the Police 'P' Division Band and included new tunes by the bandmaster G. Fred Evans – *Dulwich Village Rose*, *East Dulwich* and *The Jolly P's of Peckham*.

The decision to build the baths was not a sudden idea. It was part of a long established movement during the nineteenth century to persuade as many local authorities as possible to build public baths and wash-houses in their areas.

The story of the baths is told in *Making a Splash: The History of Dulwich Baths* by Polly Bird.

Dulwich Baths as they were decorated for the Coronation in 1953.

A game being played at Dulwich Hamlet football ground in 1951.

Dulwich Hamlet Football Club

The first known reference to the Dulwich Hamlet Football Club was in the *South London Press* on 18 February 1893. The paper carried a report that: 'A meeting of the old boys of the Hamlet Board School was held to discuss the formation of a "Dulwich Hamlet Old Boys' Club".' The report stated: 'The formation of various clubs was discussed, and immediate steps were taken respecting cricket and swimming, to be followed in due course by field, football and kindred clubs.' Sixty old boys attended the meeting and many more had written to support the idea. Lorraine Wilson and the Revd G. W. Daniell (Dulwich Old College) both accepted the position of patrons. Mr W. Brenchley (after whom Brenchley Gardens were named) was appointed as president. In the early days the team played on a ground in Woodwarde Road. The pitch was muddy and uneven. Changing rooms were some distance away at the Old Grammar School.

In 1907 the Club was elected to the Isthmian League. In the inter-war period the Club won the FA Amateur Cup four times.

The Club moved to Freeman's Ground close to Dog Kennel Hill in 1902 before moving to the neighbouring ground in 1912. A new ground was opened in 1931. This was totally rebuilt in 1992.

Ten
River Crossings

Tower Bridge

Tower Bridge is one of the world's most famous bridges and a popular tourist attraction open 360 days a year. The bridge, erected over a century ago, cost £1,184,000 and was built by 432 construction workers; tragically ten were killed whilst working on the bridge. Around fifty different designs for the new bridge were submitted and the Chamber of Commerce staged an exhibition of them; the design by Sir Horace Jones was chosen.

The opening of the new bridge was spectacular. All over it and round about there were flags and bunting, flowers and crimson cloth, as far as the eye could see. The river too was awash with vessels, big and small – barges, sail boats and steamships – many booked weeks in advance by those keen to catch the best view.

All eyes were on the carriage carrying the Prince and Princess of Wales as they drove from Buckingham Palace. When they arrived at the new bridge it was to the sound of string music from the band of the Royal Artillery. The Prince of Wales, on behalf of his mother, solemnly turned a special silver cup that was mounted on a pedestal and linked to the hydraulic equipment, and declared the bridge open. On that day a speaker at Tower Hill expressed his delight at the prospect of the Prince of Wales meeting an untimely death by falling into the river below – and received six months' imprisonment for expressing such murderous thoughts in public!

Tower Bridge a few weeks before it opened on 30 June 1894.

London Bridge, *c*. 1895. This is now in Arizona, USA, spanning a specially created lake. When it was demolished each stone was carefully numbered; the whole bridge was then crated, shipped across the Atlantic and rebuilt.

London Bridge

The original London Bridge was probably built of wood between AD 100 and 400 during the Roman occupation. In 1014 King Ethelred and King Olaf of Norway burnt down the bridge to divide the Danish forces. In 1091 the bridge was swept away by a gale; it was rebuilt soon afterwards but burnt down in 1136 and then reconstructed in elm.

The first stone bridge was begun in 1176 by Peter, Chaplain of St Mary Colechurch. The first mention of houses on the bridge is in 1201. Later pictorial records show it crowded with houses on both sides, three to seven storeys high. Near the Southwark end was Nonsuch House which was built entirely of wood. Pegs held it together instead of nails and in the centre of the bridge was a chapel dedicated to St Thomas Becket. The bridge had nineteen small arches and a drawbridge at the Southwark end.

The stone bridge was then replaced by the bridge pictured above. This was designed by John Rennie, the engineer who had already designed the first Southwark Bridge and the first Waterloo Bridge. His son Sir John Rennie supervised the building of the London Bridge which opened in 1831. This was then demolished to make way for the present London Bridge which was opened by Queen Elizabeth II on 16 March 1973.

The *Victorian Southwark Local History Pack* written by Christopher Culpin in association with Southwark Education and Leisure Services is an excellent resource for schools to use for stimulating interest in the rich history of Southwark. It includes the above picture.

Blackfriars Bridge

The first Blackfriars Bridge was designed by Robert Mylne and built between 1760 and 1769. It was constructed with nine semi-elliptical Portland stone arches and strongly reflected the influence of Italian engineer Giovanni Piranesi, with whom Mylne had spent much time when in Rome. The bridge was the third to span the Thames in London. It was funded by the Bridge House Estate, an institution dating from the eleventh century. Income from the land it owned (much of this in Southwark) was administered by the City.

This Thames crossing was originally named after William Pitt but after he fell out of favour with politicians it was renamed Blackfriars. In 1780 Gordon rioters broke down the toll gates and stole the money; tolls were levied until 1811.

The original bridge was replaced with the present one between 1864 and 1869, which was designed by Joseph Cubitt. It has five wrought-iron arches faced with cast iron on granite piers. The foundation stone was laid in 1865 by the Lord Mayor of London. The ceremony took place in a huge cofferdam on the south side of the river where a row of piles, driven closely together into the river bed and caulked like the side of a ship, formed a solid bulwark against the water. At the bottom of the dam, about 15 ft below low-water mark, the foundation stone was placed. This was a block of Cornish granite weighing over two tons.

Queen Victoria opened the bridge on the same day as Holborn Viaduct. However, at that time she was so unpopular that she and her servant, who rode behind her in the state carriage, were hissed in the Strand. The bridge was widened on the east side between 1907 and 1910.

Blackfriars Bridge, *c.* 1955.

The original Southwark Bridge, opened at midnight on 24 March 1819.

Southwark Bridge

The present Southwark Bridge was opened on 6 June 1921 by King George V. The Bishop of Southwark then pronounced a benediction on the bridge and those who had designed it.

The chief reason for rebuilding the bridge was the steepness of the gradients creating the laborious ascent of the roadway up to the centre of the old bridge. The present bridge is around 7 ft lower at that point. Another important reason for rebuilding the bridge was to make it uniform with the other bridges by building five arches instead of three to avoid a twisting course for river craft. As the Cannon Street Railway Bridge with its five openings is less than 150 yards away from Southwark Bridge it required some awkward bending of the route in order to negotiate the old bridge. Made from iron cast by Walker's of Rotherham, it was the largest bridge ever constructed with cast iron, and the undertaking was obviously too much as it sent Walker's into bankruptcy. The architect John Rennie obtained the stone from Peterhead.

Robert Stephenson described the bridge as being 'unrivalled as regards its colossal proportions, its architectural effects and the general simplicity and massive character of its details.'

The Southwark Bridge Company was formed in 1813 in response to urgent demands for a new bridge between London and Blackfriars. There was much opposition to the scheme because of the impediment created to shipping by a bridge at this narrow point in the river.

Thames Tunnel

Underground trains run on the East London Line through a famous tunnel – it was the first tunnel built under the River Thames.

The Thames Tunnel from Rotherhithe to Wapping was the crowning achievement of the great engineer Sir Marc Brunel together with his famous son Isambard Kingdom Brunel. The work was started from the Rotherhithe end in 1825. Marc Brunel's invention of a tunnelling shield enabled him to make progress where earlier attempts by other engineers had failed.

Men were killed during the building of the tunnel and there were various other setbacks including flooding, subsidence and gas. Financial difficulties caused the work to be suspended for a few years.

The tunnel was a popular tourist attraction. Visitors paid to descend when it was under construction and after it had been opened. Fairs and sideshows were held there. In August 1851 it had twice as many visitors as the Great Exhibition in Hyde Park.

Marc Brunel was publicly rewarded with the first official recognition of his achievement by being knighted by Queen Victoria in 1841. His grandson, aged three, was given the honour in June of that year of becoming the first person to pass right under the river from shore to shore. He was followed by his father, his grandfather and the directors of the Thames Tunnel Company.

Brunel's engine house, in Railway Avenue, can be visited on the first Sunday of every month from 12 noon until 4 p.m. *Brunel's Tunnel and where it led* was written by Andrew Mathewson and Derek Laval.

Engraving showing Queen Victoria visiting the tunnel soon after it had opened in 1843; she walked the whole length of the tunnel.

Rotherhithe Tunnel, c. 1910.

Rotherhithe Tunnel

The London County Council, which was superseded by the Greater London Council in 1965, left a rich legacy from which thousands of people benefit including those who use the Rotherhithe Tunnel.

Parliamentary approval for the tunnel was obtained through the Thames Tunnel (Rotherhithe and Ratcliff) Act 1900. Work on the tunnel did not begin until 1904 but, prior to that year, much time and energy were spent on relocating around 1,500 people whose homes had to be demolished. A site was acquired in Swan Road (between Brunel Road and the Thames) on which large blocks of tenements were built; Winchelsea Buildings were completed in 1902 and Rye Buildings and Sandwich Buildings were finished the following year. Hythe Buildings and Seaford Buildings completed the estate.

Out of the total cost of the Rotherhithe Tunnel of over £2 million, half was spent on acquiring property for the approaches and of rehousing people who were displaced.

The tunnel was built to the plans of Sir Maurice Fitzmaurice and took four years to complete. It was built partly with a tunnelling shield and partly by the cut and cover method. It is 1,212 yards long, excluding the approaches. The top of the tunnel is 48ft below Trinity high-water mark to allow for the passage of large ships. Over the entrance to the tunnel is a steel arch which formed the cutting edge of the tunnelling shield.

The tunnel was opened in 1908 by the Prince of Wales (later King George V). It was the second tunnel to be used for road traffic under the Thames; the first was the Blackwall Tunnel opened in 1897.

Southwark Local Studies Library possesses a well-illustrated volume which E.H. Tabor, the resident engineer in charge of construction, compiled about the building of the tunnel.

Eleven
Transport

London Bridge Station

The first London passenger steam railway was the London and Greenwich, which was opened from Deptford to Spa Road on 8 February 1836 and completed to London Bridge on 14 December 1836. The Lord Mayor of London rode on the first train out of London Bridge station. Soon there were trains every quarter of an hour from 8 a.m. until 10 p.m. Fares were advertised as 'Imperial carriages one shilling, open cars sixpence'.

The first London Bridge station had only wooden platforms and no impressive buildings. A more substantial station was built in Italianate style between 1840 and 1844, to a design by Henry Roberts. In 1849 it was rebuilt by Samuel Beazley in two parts – one side for the South Eastern Railway, which had taken over the Greenwich Railway, and the other for the remaining companies which had amalgamated to form the London, Brighton and South Coast Railway.

Pictures of the station are included in *South London Line* and *London Bridge to East Croydon* by Vic Mitchell and Keith Smith.

London Bridge station in the winter of 1913/14. The station was very badly damaged in the Second World War and was rebuilt in the 1970s.

Peckham Rye station, c. 1892.

Peckham Rye Station

The ornate Peckham Rye station, in Italian Renaissance style, is hidden behind shops which The Peckham Society would like to see demolished so a piazza can be created. When the station was built, carriages could pull off Rye Lane and on to the forecourt.

The London, Chatham & Dover Railway was the first company to run trains to Peckham. On 1 December 1865 a station opened for steam trains running between Ludgate Hill and Crystal Palace. The London, Brighton & South Coast Railway opened the South London Line on 13 August 1866. This provided a service between London Bridge and Loughborough Park (renamed East Brixton in 1894) via Old Kent Road (renamed Old Kent Road and Hatcham on 1 February 1870), Peckham (renamed Queen's Road, Peckham, on 1 December 1866) and Peckham Rye. Services were extended to Victoria on 1 May 1867.

The elaborate design of Peckham Rye station is distinctly in the London, Brighton and South Coast mould, and this is confirmed in the original plans which still exist. The building has been attributed to C.H. Driver, but the only signatures on the plans are those of the LBSC Chief Engineer, R. Jacomb Hood, and a mysterious Jackson Shand, who may have been the contractor.

A *Descriptive Account of Peckham and Camberwell Illustrated*, published in 1892 and which included the above picture, stated: 'Few suburbs in London are so well supplied with travelling accommodation as Peckham. There are trams and buses galore; while three railway companies have stations in the vicinity. It is no wonder then that it should be a favourite place of residence among those whose vocations call them daily to the city...'

Denmark Hill Station

This station, close to the King's College and Maudsley Hospitals, was opened on 13 August 1866 long before the hospitals were built. It was opened to serve mainly as a commuter station on the line between Victoria and London Bridge. Main line trains from Victoria ran through it but didn't stop.

The station was designed by W. Jacomb Hood and was built, unusually, to straddle the lines which made it visible from all sides. This seems to have inspired the architect, for he produced a building rather like the regency pavilion in Brighton. It had very fine domed roofs at each end and a splendid central pavilion which was kitted out with mahogany seats and open fireplaces, with two ticket offices for the two railway companies that used the station. One was the London, Brighton and South Coast Railway which undertook the building of the station. The other was the London, Chatham and Dover Railway.

Sadly, in 1980 the station was set alight by vandals who were never caught. The central pavilion was very badly burnt. The roof was destroyed and the walls were damaged.

The Camberwell Society, Southwark Environment Trust and British Rail worked together to restore the station and included a new pub – the Phoenix and Firkin – in the plans. This was opened on 5 June 1984. The whole project was supported by John Betjeman, Poet Laureate, who described Denmark Hill station as 'a very fine Victorian thing, a monument to South London prosperity'.

A steam train passes through Denmark Hill station in May 1959.

South Bermondsey station, 1954.

South Bermondsey Station

South Bermondsey is one of the stations on the South London Line connecting Victoria and London Bridge. It was built on the site of the original centre track and was opened on 17 June 1928 when the old station closed. The original station opened on 13 August 1866 and was known as Rotherhithe. The name was changed to South Bermondsey and 'Rotherhithe' became a station on the East London Line from 7 December 1869.

The South London Line was a product of the early competition between the railway companies that emerged in the second half of the nineteenth century. The story started when the Great Exhibition moved from Hyde Park to Sydenham in 1853.

The London, Brighton and South Coast Railway (LBSCR) jealously guarded its monopoly on traffic to the site, which was close to Sydenham and Penge stations on the London Bridge to Brighton line. It constructed a loop from Sydenham to a new Crystal Palace station, which opened in 1854.

Its rivals, the London, Chatham and Dover Railway, wanting a share of this traffic, backed a proposal by the Crystal Palace and South London Junction Railway to build a new line to Crystal Palace from Victoria via Camberwell (Denmark Hill), Peckham, Nunhead, Honor Oak and Sydenham. But the LBSCR wanted to link its London Bridge and Victoria stations. The railway companies decided to co-operate and so the South London Line came into being.

A few years ago the line became neglected but as a result of effective campaigning by the South London Link Travellers' Association (SoLLTA) the line has been given a fresh lease of life. *The SoLLTA Story* gives a history of the line.

Lordship Lane Station

Lordship Lane station was on the line from Nunhead to Crystal Palace (High Level) station which closed in 1954 after eighty-nine years' service.

French impressionist artist Camille Pissarro painted a view of the station from the old Cox's Walk footbridge. The picture is owned by the Courtauld Gallery, Somerset House, and shows a double armed signal post on the down platform, prior to the building of the signal box.

The station was demolished after the last train ran through in 1954. Over thirty years later *Peckham Society News* published a short article entitled *Major tourist attraction that never was!* 'Imagine boarding a steam train at Peckham Rye Station, chugging along to Nunhead, and then steaming past One Tree Hill and Horniman Gardens, under the bridge at Cox's Walk, through Sydenham Hill Woods until Crystal Palace High Level Station is reached. Sadly, no one had the vision of a future money-spinner when the Nunhead to Crystal Palace (High Level) line was closed in 1954. If only the clock could be turned back – but it can't! Houses and flats have been built where the railway tracks were laid in the 1860s.'

A leaflet called *From the Nun's Head to the Screaming Alice* gives details of a green walk along the former route of the Nunhead to Crystal Palace line.

This 1922 photograph reveals some of the intricate architectural detail that was demanded by the Estates Governors of Alleyn's College of God's Gift on whose land the Lordship Lane station was constructed.

Spa Road station, c. 1905.

Spa Road Station

The London and Greenwich Railway was the first passenger train service to be built in London. At first many people travelled on it for its novelty. In 1836 something like 'railway mania' hit London.

When Col Landman was asked to design the railway he decided that the tracks should be raised above the ground to the height of a two-storey house. It is not totally clear why he made that decision but even in those days there were many streets in Bermondsey which had to be crossed by the railway. Perhaps he was worried about the risk of trains colliding with cattle on the tracks because 150 years ago a lot of land beyond Bermondsey was used for grazing.

A viaduct of 878 brick arches was built to carry the railway over open country from London to Greenwich and was the first of its kind to be built.

Deptford is London's oldest passenger station; it opened on 8 February 1836. The first section of line ran to Spa Road, Bermondsey, which was the temporary terminus until 14 December 1836 when London Bridge station was opened.

When the London and Croydon railway was built in 1839, the two lines joined at Corbett's Lane. To prevent two trains from crashing, it was here that the first signal box in the world was erected. White and red lights were used at night and the signal box was sometimes known as the 'lighthouse'.

Spa Road station was closed in 1915 but the words 'Booking Office' can still be seen under the arches in Priter Way.

Steam Buses

In 1911 the National Steam Car Co Ltd opened a garage at Nos 20-26 Nunhead Lane. Its large white double deck steam buses were fired by paraffin and plied between Dulwich and Shepherds Bush; another route served Peckham and Hampton Court. However, owing to the rising cost of paraffin, the fleet was withdrawn in 1919.

In *A Historical Tour of Nunhead and Peckham Rye* Ron Woollacott included his drawing of the steam bus garage and told the story of its uses after the short life of steam buses came to an end. In 1919 the garage was taken over by the London General Omnibus Company. It was acquired in 1933 by the London Transport Passenger Board. In 1954 the garage was closed as an operational unit but was used for some time for the maintenance of vehicles.

The premises were subsequently acquired by Banfield's Luxury Coaches in 1958. The late Charles Banfield, who founded his charabanc business in 1926, had worked at Nunhead as a driver for the London General.

Some scenes from the popular TV series *On the Buses* were filmed at Nunhead. The old garage became a warehouse for drinks and was demolished in 1999. A replica of the clock tower stands close to Banfield Road.

One of the buses belonging to the National Steam Car Co. Ltd.

Trams approach St Peter's church in Lordship Lane.

Electric Trams

Electric trams were introduced to East Dulwich in 1906 with a service along Lordship Lane terminating at Barry Road. In 1907 a branch from Goose Green along East Dulwich Road terminated at Peckham Rye (Stuart Road). A further extension from Barry Road along Lordship Lane to Forest Hill was operational at the end of 1908.

A local resident who died in 1999 aged ninety-eight, Lilian Burden, remembered seeing a horse helping to pull electric trams up the steep Dog Kennel Hill – a fact not recorded in London's Transport Museum Library at Covent Garden.

The tracks on Dog Kennel Hill were quadrupled in 1912 so that the service could be improved and safety maintained. No trams were allowed to follow each other on the same line. Although other instances of four-line tracks occurred in the British Isles, Dog Kennel Hill was the only permanent arrangement which has earned it a place in transport history.

After slight changes were made to routes during the electric tram era, the trams running down Dog Kennel Hill were Nos 56 and 84 via East Dulwich Road to Peckham Rye; No. 58 via Lordship Lane to Blackwall Tunnel; No. 60 to Dulwich Library and 62 via Lordship Lane to Forest Hill.

The trams ceased running on 6 October 1951. Some time after that a roundabout was constructed at the junction of Lordship Lane and East Dulwich Road using tram setts – granite paving blocks. These still exist.

Dulwich Toll Gate

This is the only toll gate still in use in the London area; the majority were abolished by Act of Parliament in 1864. The exact date of its installation is not known.

Unlike most of the toll gates, the Dulwich one was not erected by a Turnpike Trust, but by an individual. John Morgan, Lord of the Manor of Penge, made up the road from the top of the hill to reach two fields he had rented from Dulwich College. In 1789 he was allowed to charge tolls on people passing through his fields. After his death the College kept the toll gate, and his toll gate cottage, and continued to charge tolls for the upkeep of the road.

Public tenders for collecting tolls ended in 1901, after which the Estates Governors maintained the charges of: 3d per car per return journey; 3d per horse, mule or donkey drawing a cart (2d not drawing); 10d for beasts per score, and $2\frac{1}{2}$d for sheep, lambs or hogs per score.

The explanation for why cyclists were exempt from tolls was given in the *South London Press* in 1897: 'For a considerable time each cyclist was charged 2d. This charge is not tabulated on the board; its origin is "wrop in mystery". The impost was the cause of much annoyance and many altercations. It is said that a man with a Kodak took a snapshot picture of a wrangle with a cyclist at the gate. The Governors could imagine from the expression the language used, and now cyclists go free.'

Dulwich toll gate in College Road, *c.* 1890.

Peckham Rovers Bicycle Club, still in existence around 1900.

The Popularity of Cycling

This cheap way to travel goes back to the nineteenth century. Peckham's oldest firm still in existence, A.E. Wilson's cycle firm in the High Street, started in Hill Street in around 1870. The present shop, from which it has traded for over a century, was opened in 1882. The firm's founder was Harold Wilson who traded under the name of H. Wilson & Son. The firm's name was then changed to A.E. Wilson by the founder's son.

The firm used to make 'Courier' cycles, of which they built various models. In 1903 their bicycles cost £10 or £12; a tandem was priced at £18 18s or £21. The firm also made a 'Courier' motor bicycle which cost £40.

The shop in Peckham High Street was taken over by A.E. Wilson's son, Norman Arthur Wilson, who ran it until shortly before he died, aged ninety-one, on 1 April 1995.

A cycling club, The Surrey Wheelers C.C., began in Peckham. Its inaugural meeting was held on 9 February 1886. The club's headquarters were at the Hotel & Restaurant, No. 16 Rye Lane. The club was still in existence in 1906.

In an effort to encourage more people to cycle, Southwark Council has produced a free cycling map.

Peckham Canal

The Peckham Pulse (Britain's first Healthy Living Centre), the highly acclaimed Peckham Library and the impressive arch at Peckham Square stand a few yards away from where barges berthed in the Peckham branch of the Grand Surrey Canal, opened in 1826.

The canal was used for transporting bulky goods such as road metal, coal, timber and other building materials. The canal was busy while Peckham expanded during the nineteenth century when hundreds of new houses were built After the canal was cut, the gardens of the Hill Street villas came down to its banks. Private pleasure boats and punts drifted to and fro on long summer evenings. The Boat House did a good trade in hired boats used by the young men and women of the village.

In Postman's Park in Aldersgate there are memorial plaques commemorating people who died in heroic circumstances. One plaque says 'Richard Farris, Labourer, was drowned in attempting to save a poor girl who had thrown herself into the Canal at Globe Bridge, Peckham, May 20 1878.' Globe Bridge, built in 1872, is now known as Commercial Way Bridge.

Another reminder of the canal is Whitten Timber Ltd. Mr W.H. Whitten moved his business in 1921 to Canal Head. He had started trading two years earlier from his home by selling second-hand timber, doors, windows etc. from London County Council schools that were being replaced by more modern buildings. His business prospered so he moved to premises at the side of the canal and began trading in imported softwoods.

One of the last barges in the Peckham branch of the Grand Surrey Canal is seen below in 1972. Floating in the water, on the left, is a Whitten Timber sign which pointed from a small stall at the top of Canal Head where offcuts were sold to a sales office 20 yards away. Strangely, the sign in the canal points to where Whitten's new premises are due to open at the end of 2001.

The timber-carrying barge *Bromlock* at Peckham Canal in 1972.

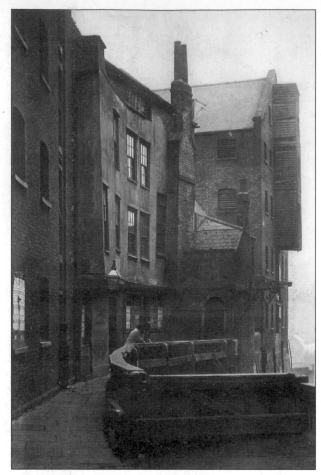

St Mary Overie's Dock in 1881.

St Mary Overie's Dock

Since Roman times, the River Thames has been used as a highway for trade. The entry for Southwark in the *Domesday Book*, compiled in 1086, mentions 'tolls on the riverbank' and 'the tideway where ships are moored' which was probably St Mary Overie's Dock. The dock took its name from the priory church which is now Southwark Cathedral.

Until a few years ago, the dock had a notice which read, 'St Mary Overie's Dock: This dock is a Free Landing Place at which the parishioners of St Saviour's Parish are entitled to Land Goods Free of Toll'.

Moored in the dock today is a replica of Sir Francis Drake's sixteenth century ship, the *Golden Hinde*. Drake tried unsuccessfully to find the north-west passage and finally returned to England via the Cape of Good Hope. He landed at Plymouth in 1580 after being the first English person to make a voyage around the world. He was knighted the following year by Queen Elizabeth I on board the *Golden Hinde* at Deptford.

In 1998 a plaque commemorating the legend of Mary Overie was unveiled when a new section of the Riverside Walkway near Southwark Bridge was officially opened. The ceremony was accompanied by cannon fire from the *Golden Hinde*.